Einstein's Explanation

of the

Unexplainable

Copyright @ 2022 Jeffrey O'Callaghan
ASIN: B0BF2ZL7MT
ISBN-13: 9798352316597

Contents

Forward...6

Article 1 Could Gravitational Time Dilation Be Responsible for Dark Energy?..9

Article 2 Einstein's explanation of the quantum properties of Electron Diffraction. 14

Article 3 Can the Geometry of Space-time be Responsible for the Evolution of a Quantum System?...18

Article 4 Explaining Mass and its Resistance to Acceleration in Terms of the Field Properties of Space-time. 21

Article 5 Quantum Entanglement as Define by Einstein................23

Article 6 Understanding the Uncertainty Principal in Terms of the dynamics of Space-time. 30

Article 7 How Should We Define Reality?.......................................37

Article 8 Defining the Probabilistic World of Quantum Mechanics in Terms of the Determinism Space-time.......................................42

Article 9 Using Einstein's Theories to Derive the Quantum Properties of a Photon...47

Article 10 Entanglement Gives Us a Way to Experimentally Determine Why the Universe Is What It Is. 52

Article 11 Using Einstein's Theories to Explain and Predict Dark Matter. 59

Article 12 Understanding Gravity the Particle and Wave Properties of Electromagnetic Energy in Terms of geometry of Space-time. 66

Article 13 Why the Future Is What It Is. 74

NArticle 14 An Alternative Explanation for the Variations in the Cosmic Background Radiation...78

Article 15 Integrating Gravity into Quantum Electrodynamics or QED in terms of the Field Properties of Space-time. 83

Article 16 Deriving the Probability Amplitudes of Quantum Mechanics in terms of the Dynamics of Space-time. 87

Article 17 The CATASTROPHIC THEORETICAL Errors in the Big Bang Theory. 91

Article 18 Should We Allow Mathematics to be the Only Definition of Reality? 97

Article 19 Karl Popper on Falsifiability. 101

Article 20 The Realty Behind the Wave Function in terms of space-time. 106

Article 21 The Double Slit Experiment in Space-time. 112

Article 22 Why the Laws of Physics do not Break Down in a Black Hole? 118

Article 23 The Effect Gravity has on the geometry of Space-time Inside a Black Hole. 123

Article 24 Why the graviton is so hard to detect in terms of space-time. 128

Article 25 A Possible Solution to the Problems of Quantum Computing. 132

Article 26 Could the Energy Density of a Collapsing Universe Be Responsible the beginning of our universe? 137

Article 27 Einstein's Block Universe Fact or Fiction? 142

Article 28 Quantum Tunneling in Space-time. 146

Article 29 A Classical Reason why energy is quantized in terms of the observable properties of our universe. 151

Article 30 Quantum Superpositioning Explained in Terms of Space-time. 156

Article 31 Why the Arrow of Time is Irreversible. 158

Article 32 Should We Allow Mathematics to Be the Only Definition of Reality?..................161

Article 33 Should Allow Mathematics to Define Our Understanding of the Universe or Have it Define Our Mathematics?..................165

Article 34 Defining Quantum Gravity in terms of an emergent property of space-time..................169

Article 35 Why Finding a Theory of Everything is so Difficult...172

Article 36 Reality Is What It Is Not What Mathematics tell us It Can Be..................176

Article 37 Why Our Universe is Asymmetrical With Respect to Time and the Laws of Physics..................180

Article 38 Particle spins in terms of four-dimensional space-time..................183

Article 39 *Why an electron does not fall into the nucleus in terms of the strong and weak nuclear forces*..................189

Article 40 A background independent quantum gravity in terms of Relativity..................195

Article 41 Defining Quantum gravity in terms of an emergent property of space-time..................198

Article 42 What supports the geometry of "empty" space-time?..................200

Article 43 A Classical explanation of the delayed choice quantum eraser experiment in terms of space-time..................202

Article 44 Merging the properties of Quantum Mechanics and Relativity to resolve the measurement problem..................213

Article 45 Defining Maxwells Equation in terms of the physical properties of space-time..................218

Article 46 The Casmir effect in space-time..................225

Article 47 Einstein's solution to the horizon problem..................228

Article 48 Could Einstein's realization energy can only be propagated at the speed of light solves the Flatness problem.233

Sources..238

Forward

There are many observations that appear to be unexplainable by modern theories, such as the existence of dark matter and energy. However, as these previously published Articles by the author suggests this might not be.

For example, Article 1 "Could gravitational time dilation be responsible for Dark Energy?" shows how Einstein, if he had been aware of its existence before he died could have used his theoretical prediction that time is dilated or slowed by gravity to define its casualty in a manner that is consistent with all observational data associated with it. This in turn would have given him the ability to define what Dark Matter is.

Another place where modern theories break down is defining why our observable reality is what it is. For example, many feel that Quantum Theory is the only one that gives a plausible explanation of the double slit experiment by assuming waves exhibit particle-like properties and particles exhibit wave-like ones.

However, that is not consistent with how most of us perceive our observable world and opposes classical, Newtonian and Relativistic Physics.

Yet, as the Article 22 "The double slit experiment in space-time" shows Einstein gave us a classical reason why its results are what they are in a manner consistent with his theory and the observable properties of our universe.

Please remember when reviewing these articles that they are all interrelated. If you feel that one does not a provide an answer to all of your questions, please take a second to review the others because you will find it there.

Even though there is a lot of work left to do the author feels these articles, when put together, will produce a solid foundation for the long sought-after Universal Field Theory by defining all the observable properties of the universe including those of a quantum environment in terms of a relativistic one and a relativistic environment in terms of a quantum one.

**Everything should be made
as simple as possible,
but not simpler.
Albert Einstein**

Article 1
Could Gravitational Time Dilation Be Responsible for Dark Energy?

On 8 January 1998, researchers announced the startling discovery that the universe's expansion is accelerating due to what is has come to be called Dark Energy. Another team, the High-Z Supernova Search Team, independently confirmed the discovery soon after. Until then, most astronomers had thought that cosmic expansion should be slowing due to the gravitational attraction among stars, galaxies, and other matter.

There are several explanations for it including it is a property of space or a result of its quantum properties.

Another possibility is that Einstein's theory of gravity is not correct.

However, one possibility that **may** have been overlooked is that it is **direct result** of the slowing of time by gravity as defined in his General Theory of Relativity.

Einstein told us and it has been confirmed by observations of matter falling into black holes, the rate at which time passes is perceived to be slower in all environments where the gravitational potential is greater with respect to where it is being observed. This means the further we look back in time, where it was greater due to the more densely pack matter and energy, the estimate of its rate of expansion would appear to be **slower** when observed from the present than it actually was if that were not taken into consideration.

This is because as Steven Weinberg the noble prize-winning physicists pointed out Einstein equation $E=mc^2$ tells us energy and mass are equivalent.

Therefore, to define the total gravitational potential of a volume of space-time one must NOT only consider that given by its mass but all forms of energy encapsulated in it.

This suggests if the slowing of time caused by the differential gravitational potential between the past and the present was not taken into account the universe would have been expanding **faster** in the past than it would appear to be from the present.

However, because energy can neither be created or destroyed the total mass/energy content of the universe must remain constant throughout its history while its density depends only on its volume. This means, the time dilation with respect to the present at each point in its history due to the slowing effects of gravity could be estimated solely on its differential volume between the past and present.

We also we know that gravity has a slowing effect on the universe's expansion and as the density of matter decreases due to its increasing volume the rate of that slowing also decreases.

Therefore, the rate of its expansion would be faster than it would appear to be from the perspective of the present due to the effects gravity has on time while the rate of its slowing would be declining due to its decreasing effect of its gravitational potential has on the universe's expansion as its volume increases.

This means because the gravitational potential was greater in the past, the observations suggesting the universe's expansion is accelerating may be the result of the effects gravity has on time which would make it **appear** to be expanding slower in the past that it actually was. This means it **may** have been expanding faster in the past than it is now.

Yet, if the effects of these processes is non-linear there will be a point in its history where one **may** appear to overtake the other.

One could justify further research by using the observation mentioned earlier that about 5 billion years ago the universe's expansion appears to be accelerating because one could use Einstein theories to define when that should have occurred.

For example, one could derive the actual rate of its expansion in the past by using Einstein equations to determine the change in the relative magnitude of the universe's gravitational potential in the past with respect to present then determine the magnitude of the time dilation it would have caused based on how its volume has changed. One could then use that to determine the magnitude of the time dilatation and the universe's expansion rate between the past and the present caused by it. This would give us more accurate estimate of the **actual** rate of its expansion in the past with respect to the present.

If it was found, its expansion rate before 5 billion years ago was **actually** faster than it is now it would suggest that its expansion is **not** accelerating but still decelerating and would support the above conjecture.

Some may say the slowing of time due to gravity would not affect our perception of its expansion. However, Einstein tells us the timing of events that cause the universe to expand is locked in the past along with its gravitational potential at the time that expansion took place. Therefore, one **must** take it into account when defining its expansion.

If that was not done it MAY have resulted in giving us the perception the universe expansion is accelerating even though it is not.

Article 2
Einstein's explanation of the quantum properties of Electron Diffraction.

Currently there are two primary ways science attempts to explain and define the behavior of our universe. The first is Quantum Mechanics or the branch of physics which use the mathematics of the wave function to define the evolution of particles in terms of a one-dimensional point. The other is Einstein relativistic one which defines it in terms of an electromagnetic wave.

However, physics is an observational science whose purpose is **not** only to explain what we observe, like the position of a particle but why we obverse what we do.

Therefore, the creditability of Quantum Mechanics should **not only** depend on predicting where a particle is when observed but how quantum system evolves to the point where is it observed.

Yet, the observation that particles such as an electron can be diffracted means one of its fundamental assumptions, that a particle can be defined as a one-dimensional point is falsified. This because it is impossible to explain that observation in terms of a point particle that has no volume. Therefore, because one of its fundamental assumptions is observational shown to be incorrect, we have no choice but to look for another way of explaining of why a particle position is observed to be where it is.

Additionally, the process of refraction falsifies another one its core principle, that the wave function **always** collapses to a particle when it interacts with an observer or its external environment. Therefore, the fact that refraction involves the interaction of the wave function with a diffracting medium such as a prism falsifies that principal because it does not collapse to a particle when it first contacts it but continues as a wave even after it exits This has been experimentally confirmed by the fact the energy can maintain its wave properties after undergoing success consecutive diffractions through prisms.

However, one can explain how and why a particle can be diffracted and quantized at the same time in terms of Einstein theories.

One can accomplish this by using the observations provided by the science of wave mechanics and those of a space-time environment defined by Einstein's relativistic theories.

For example, the science of wave mechanics along with the observations of a relativistic environment tell us wave energy moves continuously through space-time unless it is prevented from doing so by someone or something interacting with it. This would result in its energy being confined to three-dimensional space. The science of wave mechanics also tells us the three-dimensional "walls" of this confinement will result in its energy being reflected back on itself thereby creating a resonant or standing wave in three-dimensional space. This would cause its wave energy to be concentrated at the point in space were a particle would be found. Additionally, wave mechanics also tells us the energy of a resonant system, such as a standing wave can only take on the discrete or quantized values associated with its fundamental or a harmonic of its fundamental frequency.

This means if an electromagnetic wave is prevented from moving through space either by being observed or encountering an object it is reduced or "Collapses" to a form a standing wave that would define the quantized energy quantum theory associates with a particle.

However, it also tells us the reason a wave remains when it interacts with a prism is because it is redirected **not** prevented from moving through it. This as mentioned earlier is a direct contradiction of the quantum mechanical assumption that when the wave properties a quantum environment interact with its environment including a prism it takes the form of a particle.

Yet, this also tells us a particle would occupy an extended volume of space defined by the wavelength associated with its standing wave. This tells us the reason particles such as an electron can be diffracted is because their standing wave component can interact with its environment in terms of the observable properties of ours which as mentioned earlier Quantum theory cannot.

As was mentioned earlier, physics is an observational science whose purpose is **not** only to explain what we observe, like the position of a particle but why we obverse what we do.

Therefore, what we as physicists and mathematicians **must** decide is should we allow the mathematics of the wave function to define our understanding of reality because it is possible a new system of math based on the behavior of observable properties of "our world" could open doors to new technologies that will enable our civilization to advance beyond were one based solely on Quantum Mechanics can.

Article 3
Can the Geometry of Space-time be Responsible for the Evolution of a Quantum System?

Quantum Mechanics defines the evolution of its environment in terms of the mathematical properties of a wave function. Additionally, it assumes a quantum system exists simultaneously as both a wave and particle and **only** becomes a particle when it interacts with its external world. However, it cannot tell us how or why that happens in terms of our observable environment.

On the other hand, Einstein defines the evolution of a space-time environment in terms of the observable properties of an electromagnetic wave.

Therefore, to define how the geometry of space-time is responsible for the evolution of a quantum system one must show how and why the interactions of an electromagnetic wave with a space-time environment causes it to **appear** to exist simultaneously as both waves and particles.

To do that we must first establish a connection between a quantum and the space-time environment as defined by Einstein. This can be accomplished because the evolution of both is defined by a wave.

For example, Relativity defines evolution of space-time in terms of the energy propagated by electromagnetic wave while that of a Quantum system is defined in terms of the mathematics of a wave function.

This commonality suggests the wave function **may** be a mathematical representation of an electromagnetic wave in space-time environment.

One can use this commonality, the science of wave mechanics and the space-time geometry defined by Einstein to explain why it is responsible for the evolution of a quantum environment.

This because they tell us an electromagnetic wave would move continuously through it unless it is prevented from doing so by someone or something interacting with it. This would result in it being confined to three-dimensional space. The science of wave mechanics also tells us the three-dimensional "walls" of this confinement will result in its energy being reflected back on itself thereby creating a resonant or standing wave in three-dimensional space. This would cause its energy to be concentrated at the point in space were that occurred.

Additionally, wave mechanics also tells us the energy of a resonant system such as a standing wave can only take on the discrete or quantized values associated with its fundamental or a harmonic of its fundamental frequency. This explains why in terms of the wave properties of a space-time environment energy is always quantized when observed in a manner which is consistent with the description of the environment defined by Quantum Mechanics.

This also provides a Classical mechanism which can explain one of the core principals Quantum Mechanics in that when wave properties of light and all other forms of energy are prevented from moving through space either by being observed or encountering an object that energy will become quantized in the form of a particle.

Additionally, it also tells us energy is NOT simultaneously propagated as both a wave and particle but instead is done so as either one of the other but not simultaneously at the same time.

Article 4
Explaining Mass and its Resistance to Acceleration in Terms of the Field Properties of Space-time.

Mass is both a property of a physical body and a measure of its resistance to acceleration when a force is applied.

The Higgs boson was discovered at the CERN Particle Physics Laboratory near Geneva, Switzerland, in 2012, which, according to the Standard Model of particle physics is what gives all other fundamental particles mass.

However, despite the work of thousands of researchers around the world, nobody has been able to explain exactly how it does that or why some particles are more massive than others.

However, there is another way to understand mass and its resistance to acceleration based solely on the field concepts of Einstein's theories.

For example, Einstein defined the physicality of mass in terms of the energy density associated with a displacement in space-time which he quantified by the equation $E=mc^2$. This means he also defined the reason why some particles are heavier than others are because they have a greater energy content and therefore a greater displacement in space-time than other particles. Therefore, the equation E=mc^2 not only defines physicality of mass but also quantifies why some particles are heavier that others in terms of the field properties of space-time.

However, he also told us the rate at which energy can be propagated is constant and limited by the speed of light. This suggests, according to Relativity, the reason why mass resists acceleration is because the speed at which energy can be added to it is limited by the speed of light.

This means the acceleration of a mass would ALWAYS be proportional to the energy content associated with its mass.

This suggest the reason the resistance mass has to acceleration **may** not be related to the field properties of a Higgs boson but the fact that the speed of light limits rate at which energy at to it.

This means one does not need the Higgs boson to explain mass and why it resists a change in motion because one can use the **observable** properties of our environment and field properties of Einstein's theories to do so.

Article 5
Quantum Entanglement as Define by Einstein.

Presently, there is disconnect between our understanding of one of the most mysterious facets of Quantum Mechanics, that of quantum entanglement and the classical one of separation.

Entanglement occurs when two particles are linked together no matter their separation from one another. Quantum Mechanics assumes even though these entangled particles are not physically connected, they are still able to interact or share information with each other instantaneously.

Many believe this means the universe does not live by the classical laws of separation or those derived by Einstein, which state that no information can be transmitted faster than the speed of light.

However, we must be careful not to jump to conclusions because Einstein gave us a definitive answer as to how and why some particles, such as photons are entangled while others may not be in terms of the physical properties of space-time.

Quantum Mechanics assumes that entanglement occurs when two particles or molecules share on a quantum level one or more properties such as spin, polarization, or momentum. This connection persists even if you move one of them far away from the other. Therefore, when an observer interacts with one the other is instantly affected.

There is irrefutable experimental evidence the act of measuring the state of one of a pair of photons can instantaneously affect another even though they are physically separated from each other.

However, before we come to the conclusion it is a result of their quantum mechanical properties, we should first examine the experimental setup and any variables that may allow us to come to a different conclusion.

(This description was obtained from the Live Science web site.) One of the experiments many assume verifies that entanglement is a quantum phenomenon uses a laser beam fired through a certain type of crystal which causes individual photons to be split into pairs of entangled photons. The photons can be separated by a large distance, hundreds of miles or even more. When observed, Photon A takes on an up-spin state. Entangled Photon B, though now far away, takes up a state relative to that of Photon A (in this case, a down-spin state). The transfer of state (or information) between Photon A and Photon B takes place at a speed of at least 10,000 times the speed of light, possibly even instantaneously, regardless of distance. Scientists have successfully demonstrated quantum entanglement with photos, electrons, molecules of various sizes, and even very small diamonds).

However, Einstein told us there are no preferred reference frames by which one can measure distance.

Therefore, he tells the distance between the observation points in a laboratory, can also be defined from the perspective of the photons in the above experiment.

(Some have suggested that if you have two photons moving in opposite directions, you can only treat one as being stationary at a time, not both simultaneously" However that directly contradicts Relativity because it means that from the perspective of the stationary one the lab is moving at the speed of light away from it while the other one is moving at the speed of light in the opposite direction from the lab. However, that would mean the second photon is moving at twice the speed of light from the perspective of the first one which according to Relativity is not possible.

The only way to resolve this issue is to assume that from their perspective they are each moving at half speed of light with respect to the laboratory where they were entangled.

One can understand how Einstein's may have viewed this by using his concept of light cones. This is because their light cones are expanding at the speed of light while each photon is moving away from their point of origin at the speed of light. This tells from their prospective their light cones, their worldlines will always be causality connected along the spacetime path of the lab. However, it also tells us that each photon from the perspective of the lab will be moving in opposite directions from it a half the speed of light. This is because if one draws a perpendicular worldline from the apex of their light cone to a horizontal line through the point to where they intersect it will divide the velocity vector of each their light cones in half.)

Einstein's math and observations tell us time moves slower when an object is in relative motion and stops if it is moving at the velocity of light. Therefore, from the perspective of each photon moving at the speed of light would view time as having stopped relative to the laboratory. Therefore, because from their perspective time has stop, the information they carry from the lab would be entangled no matter how far apart they might be. This is the definition of entanglement.

The same would be true if you looked at it from the perspective of the Lorentz contractions and Einstein's math because that tells us that length contracts to zero along its velocity vector from the perspective of anything moving at the speed of light. **However, because each photon as was just mentioned is moving at half the speed of light in opposite directions from the perspective of the lab each would view the distance between the end points as being half of what it was.** However, because they are moving in the opposite directions one would have to subtract them resulting in the distance between the endpoints of the measurements again being zero. Therefore, all photons which originate from the same point will be entangled because from their perspective the distance between the end point of the measurement will be zero.

One would come to the same conclusion if they are viewed in terms of their light cones because it expands at the same velocity as they move away from their point of origin. Therefore, they will always intersect and be casually connected or entangled no matter how far apart they might be from their point of origin.

Therefore, according to Einstein's theory all photons would be entangled no matter how far they may appear to be from the perspective of an observer who is looking at them.

In other words, the entanglement of photons can be explained and predicted terms of the relativistic properties of space-time as defined by Einstein as well as by Quantum Mechanics.

One way of verifying if the entanglement of photons were due to the relativistic properties of space-time would be to determine if particles which were **not** moving at the speed of light experience entanglement over the same distances as photons do.

However, one must be careful when determining why some particles are and some are not because the wave particle duality of existence as defined by Quantum Mechanics and the fact that the wave properties of all particle has been confirmed through observations tell us that they all will have an extended volume related to their wavelength. Therefore, particles will be entangled if the distance between them is less that because they will be in physical contact with each other.

Therefore, to determine the causality of a particle's entanglement one must first determine if from their perspective they are connected. To do this one must as was mentioned earlier determine relativistic distance between them due to their relative velocities with respect to their origin. If was found that they are entangled even after that distance is greater than their extended volume it would confirm their entanglement is related to the existence of a quantum environment. However, it was found that it ceased after exceeding it, it would suggest it was relativistic property of space-time.

Therefore, if it was found that only photons experience entanglement when their observation points were separated by large distances while others which are not moving at the speed of light **do not,** it would support the idea that it is a result of the relativistic properties of space defined by Einstein and not by their Quantum mechanical properties.

This is because as was just mentioned earlier all particles will be entangled if the distance between the endpoints of their observations, after being adjusted for their relative velocity is less than their volume as defined by observations.

This provides an **experimental way** to determine if entanglement is a relativistic property of space-time or a property of a Quantum environment because if it was found that entanglement ceased when viewed from the perspective of particles moving slower than the speed of light was greater than a particle's volume as defined by their wavelength it would suggest that it is a relativistic property of space-time. However, if it was found that it did not it could only mean it was property of a quantum environment

Article 6
Understanding the Uncertainty Principal in Terms of the dynamics of Space-time.

Quantum Mechanics states what the universe is made of while not giving an explanation of why it is that way in terms of the observable properties of our universe while Relativity gives us an explanation of why it is what it is but does not tell us what it is made of.

For example, the quantum world is defined by how the mathematical properties of the wave function interact with the wave-particle duality of existence to create our universe. However, it also tells us there is an uncertainty in simultaneously defining quantities such as the momentum and position of a particle. But does **not** provide an explanation why this uncertainty exists.

On the other hand, Relativity explains the existence of the universe and the particles it contains in terms of a dynamic interaction between space and time without telling us what the wave-particle duality of existence is or how it interacts with it to create the Uncertainty Principal as defined by Quantum Mechanics.

Therefore, to understand their dynamics in terms of space-time we must first establish a connection between its observable components and the mathematical evolution of the wave function.

One can accomplish this by using the fact that Relativity defines the evolution of space-time in terms of an electromagnetic wave while, as was mentioned earlier the mathematical properties of the wave function defines how a quantum environment evolves to the point where it becomes our observable universe.

This commonality suggests the wave function could be a mathematical representation of an electromagnetic wave in space-time.

This means one **may** be able to explain the uncertainty principal associated with the wavefunction in terms of interaction between space and time.

For example, the science of wave mechanics and Relativity tell us an electromagnetic wave would move continuously through space-time unless it is prevented from doing so by being observed or something interacting with it. This would result in it being confined to three-dimensional space. The science of wave mechanics also tells us the three-dimensional "walls" of this confinement will result in its energy being reflected back on itself thereby creating a resonant or standing wave in three-dimensional space. This would cause the energy of an electromagnetic wave to be concentrated at the point in space were a particle would be found.

Additionally, wave mechanics also tells us the energy of a resonant system such as a standing wave, such as the one that earlier defined a particle can only take on the discrete or quantized values associated with its fundamental or a harmonic of its fundamental frequency.

(The boundaries or "walls" of its confinement would be defined by its wave properties. If an electromagnetic wave is prevented from moving through space-time it will be reflected back on itself. However, that reflected wave still cannot move through it therefore it will be reflected back creating a standing wave. Therefore, the wave itself defines its boundaries.)

This shows how one can explain and predict the evolution of a quantum environment **based on observations** of a relativistic one.

However, it also provides a Classical explanation for the wave particle duality of existence which is one of the core principles Quantum Mechanics because it explains why, in terms of classical mechanics if the wave properties of all forms of energy is prevented from moving through space either by being observed or encountering an object that energy will be observed in the quantized in the form of a particle.

Next, we must explain how the energy or information "volume" of a system is responsible for both the uncertainty involved in measurement of the **conjugate pairs** such as the momentum and position of an object or particle in both a relativistic and quantum environment.

As was shown earlier the energy of a particle in Quantum Mechanics is distributed over a volume associated with its wave function. While in Relativity it would be distributed over a volume of a particle associated with its standing wave component which was defined earlier.

However, the fact that both of these theories assume that energy or information of a system can nether be created or destroy provides the basis for the connecting the uncertainty principal to the space-time environment of Relativity.

This is because, both Quantum Mechanics and Relativity define the momentum and position of particles with respect to a one-dimensional point in the mathematical field of the wave function while Relativity does so with respect to the point called the center of mass of an object.

This means the accuracy as to where that point is in relation to either its information center or center of mass is directly related to how much of its energy is taken from the system to accomplish a measurement.

This means the measurement of anyone of the conjugate pairs of all systems such as the momentum or position will affect the other.

However, to measure the conjugate pairs of a system including the momentum or position in both a quantum and relativistic environment one must determine where relative to the information or energy volume of the system the measurements are being taken. Therefore, there will **always** be an uncertainty if one cannot determine where those points are with respect to it.

Therefore, because Quantum Mechanics is information driven the more accurate the measurement of the momentum of a particle the more information regarding it must be removed from it and the less is available to measure the other component of its Conjugate pair.

This makes the determination of its position more uncertain because there is less information left in its information "volume" to define it. While the more information taken out of it regarding its position will result in there being less to define its momentum. This makes this determination of its momentum more uncertain because less information left in its information "volume" to define it. This would be true for all Conjugate pairs.

However, the same would be true when measuring either the momentum or position of a particle or that of an object such as a planet system or star in a relativistic system because as was mentioned earlier its energy is also conserved. Therefore because, the accuracy of a measurement is directly related to the amount of energy available to define a system; the measurement of each component of momentum or position of a system will affect the other.

For example, the added energy required to make a more accurate measurement of a systems momentum will result in there being less to define its position. This makes the determination of its position more uncertain because there is less energy in that system to define it. While the more energy required to make a more accurate measurement of its position will result in there being less to define its momentum. This makes this determination of its momentum more uncertain because there is less energy left in the system to define it.

This explains why one cannot precisely measure both the momentum and position of objects in a relativistic environment in terms of the uncertainty principal of quantum mechanics. The reason it is unobservable is because the individual components of large objects in relativistic environment average out the uncertainty of their position and momentum of their individual comments

This shows how one can the explain the existence of the Uncertainty Principle or why the components of the conjugate pairs of particles cannot both be precisely determined at the same time in a quantum environment in terms of the dynamics of space-time.

Article 7
How Should We Define Reality?

This question is especially relevant for physicists who struggle on daily basis to define the "reality" of our universe.

Some attempt to define it **only** on the abstract mathematical analysis of an environment.

For example, Quantum Mechanics **describes** the "reality" or state of a quantum system in terms of the mathematical probability of finding it in a particular configuration when a measurement is made.

However, describing it in those terms means that each probabilistic outcome of an event can become one in the future. This is why some proponents of Quantum Mechanics assume the universe splits into multiple realities with every measurement.

This also may be one reason why Niels Bohr, the father of Quantum Mechanics said that "If Quantum Mechanics hasn't profoundly shocked you, you haven't understood it yet."

However, others **derive** it in terms of observable proprieties of our universe.

For example, Isaac Newton derived the laws of gravity by developing a mathematical relationship based on **observing** the movement of planets and the distance between them. He then derived a mathematical equation, defining a "reality" which could predict their future movements based on observations of their previous movements.

Both the probabilities of Quantum Mechanics and Newton's gravitational laws give valid descriptions of "a reality" because they allow scientists to predict future events with considerable accuracy.

However, the purpose of theoretical physics **not only** to define and predict what we observe but to **explain why** we observe what we do.

For example, at the time of their discovery Newton's gravitational laws allowed scientists to make extremely accurate predictions of planetary movements based on their previous movements, but they could not explain why those laws exist.

However, Einstein defined a different "reality" that not only could explain why they those laws existed but provided an explanation for why they are what they are.

This shows, just as there was room for an alternative "reality" which could explain them, there could be one that explains the predictive powers of Quantum Mechanics.

This is true even though many physicists feel there is no room for alternatives because modern experiments, combined with quantum theory's mathematics give us the most accurate predictions of events that have ever been achieved.

As was mentioned earlier describing "reality" **only** in terms of the probabilities as Quantum Mechanics means every possible outcome **can** become one in the future.

Yet this would **not** be true if those outcomes were the result of an interaction between a quantum environment and the physical one of our observable universe.

For example, when we role dice in a casino most do not think there are six of them out there waiting for the dice to tell us which one we will occupy after it is rolled. This is because the probability of getting a six is determined or caused by its physical interaction with the observable properties of the table in the casino where it is rolled and **not** on the probability of a specific outcome occurring. This tells us the probabilities associated with a roll of the dice does not define the casino, the casino defines those probabilities.

As was mentioned earlier Quantum Mechanics is able to quantify the observable properties of its environment but is unable to explain why those properties exists.

But that does mean we should not look for another way to do so.

For example, the science of wave mechanics and Relativity tell us an electromagnetic wave moves continuously through space-time unless it is prevented from doing so by interacting with someone or something. This would result in it being confined to three-dimensional space. The science of wave mechanics also tells us the three-dimensional "walls" of this confinement will result in its energy being reflected back on itself thereby creating a resonant or standing wave in three-dimensional space. This would cause its energy to be concentrated at the point in space were a particle would be found.

Additionally, wave mechanics also tells us the energy of a resonant system such as a standing wave can only take on the discrete or quantized values associated with its fundamental or a harmonic of its fundamental frequency that the wave function associates with a particle.

As was mentioned earlier what defines the "reality" of getting a six when rolling a dice in casino is **not** the probability of getting one but the physical properties of how the dice interacts with casino it occupies.

Similarly, what defines a quantum environment **may** not be due to the probabilities associated with the wave function but the interactions of an energy wave with the space-time properties of its environment.

This means there **may** be an alternative "reality" that can not only can explain the quantization of our observable environment but can also provide an **explanation** why that happens.

What we as theoreticians need to ask ourselves is our job only to quantify our environment as Quantum Mechanics does or should we also attempt to explain why it is what it is in terms of our observable environment.

Article 8
Defining the Probabilistic World of Quantum Mechanics in Terms of the Determinism Space-time.

Currently there are two primary ways science attempts to explain and define the behavior of our universe. The first is Quantum Mechanics or the branch of physics which defines its evolution in terms of the probabilities associated with the wave function. The other is Einstein relativistic one which defines it in terms of the deterministic properties of space and time.

Specifically, Einstein defines the evolution of a space-time environment in terms of an electromagnetic wave interacting with its environment while Quantum Mechanics uses the probabilistic interpretation of the wave function to define the most probable configuration of a system when it interacts with its environment or an observer.

Since we all live in the same world you would expect the probabilistic approach of Quantum Mechanics to be compatible with the deterministic one of Einstein.

Unfortunately, they define two different worlds which **appear** to be incompatible. One defines existence in terms of the probabilities associated with the wavefunction while the other defines it in terms of the deterministic properties of space and time.

However, even though those probabilities appear to be incompatible with Relativity's determinism it can be shown that one **may be** the **causality** of the other.

For example, when one roles dice in a casino most of us realize the probability of a six appearing is related to or caused by its physical interaction with properties of the table in the casino where it is rolled. Putting it another way what defines the casualty of a six appearing is **not** the probability of getting one but the interaction of the dice with the table and environment of the casino it occupies.

However, to understand how the probabilistic interpretation of the wave function can be caused by an interaction between it and a space-time environment one must show how and why it is responsible for them.

But before we begin, we need to establish a connection between it and the classically deterministic properties of space-time as defined by Einstein.

This can be accomplished because as was mentioned earlier in Relativity defines the evolution of space-time it terms of an electromagnetic wave interacting with its environment while the mathematics associated with wave function represents how a Quantum environment evolves to define a systems configuration when it interacts with an observer or its environment.

This suggests the wave function that governs the probabilistic evolution of a quantum environment may be a mathematical representation of deterministic properties of an electromagnetic wave that governs evolution in space-time. If true one should be able to derive both in terms of the deterministic properties of one in space-time.

For example, the science of wave mechanics along with the fact that Relativity tells us an electromagnetic wave moves continuously through space-time unless it is prevented from doing so by being observed or interacting with its environment. This would result in its energy being confined to three-dimensional space. The science of wave mechanics also tells us the three-dimensional "walls" of this confinement will result in its energy being reflected back on itself thereby creating a resonant or standing wave in three-dimensional space. This would cause its wave energy to be concentrated at the point in space were a particle would be found. Additionally, wave mechanics also tells us the energy of a resonant system, such as a standing wave can only take on the discrete or quantized values associated with its fundamental or a harmonic of its fundamental frequency.

Yet, this is similar to how Quantum Mechanics defines the evolution of its environment in the sense that its wave properties **only** become a quantized particle when observed or interacting with its environment.

(The boundaries or "walls" of its confinement would be defined by its wave properties because as was just mentioned if an electromagnetic wave is prevented from moving through space it will be reflected back on itself. However, that reflected wave still cannot move through it therefore it will be reflected back creating a standing wave.)

However, that also tells us a particle would occupy an extended volume of space defined by the wavelength of its standing wave.

This suggests what defines the fact that a particle appears where it does is **may not** be determined by probabilities associated with the wavefunction but an interaction of an electromagnetic wave with the physical properties of space-time.

However, the probabilistic interpretation of the wave function is **necessary** (in part) because Quantum Mechanics defines the position of a particle in terms of mathematical point in space which is randomly distributed with respect to a center of the standing wave which earlier defined one.

Therefore, the randomness of where that point is with respect to a particle's center will result in its position, when observed to be randomly distributed in space. This means one must define where it appears in terms of probabilities to average the deviations that are caused by the random placement of that point.

As was mentioned earlier when one roles dice in a casino most realize the probability of a six appearing is related to or caused by its physical interaction with properties of the table in the casino where it is rolled.

Similarly, one **does not** have to assume the probabilities of Quantum Mechanics defines its environment because as was shown above it **may be** caused by a deterministic property of space-time.

Article 9
Using Einstein's Theories to Derive the Quantum Properties of a Photon.

Einstein tells us particles with mass cannot move faster than the speed of light while Quantum Mechanics tells us that all energy including electromagnetic MUST be quantized and therefore it assumes it is propagated by a particle called a photon.

However, because observations of particles in particle accelerators **appears** to verify Einstein assumption that if photons had mass, they **could not** move at the speed of light one must assume they have no mass.

But if it has no mass, it also has no energy because his equation $E=mc^2$ tells us energy is equivalent to mass.

(Some have tried to use a mathematical argument the equation $E=mc^2$ is a special case of the more general equation: $E^2 = p^2c^2+m^2c^4$ which for a particle with no mass (m = 0), reduces down to $E = pc$. Therefore, because photons (particles of light) have no mass, they must obey $E = pc$ and they get all of their energy from their momentum. However, the "p" in the equation NOT ONLY represents the momentum of a photon it also represents the energy associated with its motion. Thus, according to E=mc^2 that energy **must** also be considered mass.

Some have also suggested that because "E" is the total relativistic energy, which consists of rest mass (mc^2), and momentum (pc) it is fundamentally wrong to say that anything with energy has mass. Therefore, a photon with momentum can still carry energy even if it has no rest mass.

However, momentum is defined as p = mv in Newtonian physics and in Relativity a photon moving at the speed of light would be p=mc. Therefore, it is FUNDAMENTALLY WRONG as some have suggested to say that the momentum of a photon can have ZERO mass because if it did the energy value of particle with no or 0 mass defined by p=mc would be zero.)

Putting it another way Einstein tells us it **does not matter** how we define the energy of a photon the fact that it has energy means it also has mass and therefore, **should not** be able move at the speed of light.)

Therefore, because observations of particles in particle accelerators **appears** to verify Einstein assumption that the particle called a photon **could not** carry energy at the speed of light one needs to explain how its energy can be propagated at that speed in terms of his theories.

One can use the science of wave mechanics to understand how this is possible because it tells us waves move energy from one location to another without transporting the material they are moving on. In other words, the molecules that make up a wave on water remain stationary with respect to its geometry while its energy is propagated through it.

Similarly, the energy of an electromagnetic wave can move at the speed of light because the geometric units of space-time associated with its peaks and valleys do not move the components of it laterally along it surface but **only** transmit their energy to the next one as it moves through its environment.

This explains why electromagnetic wave energy can move through it at the speed of light.

However, one can also use the science of wave mechanics to understand why an it **always** takes on the form of a particle called a photon when it interacts with an observer or its environment.

For example, wave mechanics tells us an electromagnetic wave would move continuously through space-time unless it is prevented from doing so by someone observing or something interacting with it. This would result in its energy being confined to three-dimensional space. It also tells us the three-dimensional "walls" of this confinement will result in its energy being reflected back on itself thereby creating a resonant or standing wave in three-dimensional space. This would cause its wave energy to be concentrated at the point in space were a particle would be found.

Additionally, wave mechanics also tells us the energy of a resonant system such as a standing wave can only take on the discrete or quantized values associated with its fundamental or a harmonic of its fundamental frequency.

Therefore, as was shown above assuming a photons energy is propagated by an electromagnetic wave allows one to understand why it **can move energy** at the speed of light and why it **only appears** as a photon when it interacts with its environment or an observer in a manner that is consistent with the observable properties of our environment and the assumptions of Einstein Theories.

However, it also provides a Classical explanation for one of the core principles of Quantum Mechanics because it explains why in a deterministic way, if the wave properties of all forms of energy is prevented from moving through space-time either by being observed or

encountering an object that energy will be observed in the quantized in the form of a particle.

Article 10
Entanglement Gives Us a Way to Experimentally Determine Why the Universe Is What It Is.

Entanglement provides an experimental way of determining if Quantum Mechanics or Einstein's Relativistic theories define why our universe is what it is.

This is because it is one of the core principles of quantum physics. In short it assumes two particles or molecules share on a quantum level one or more properties such as spin, polarization, or momentum. It also assumes this connection persists even if you move one of the entangled objects far away from the other. Therefore, when an observer interacts with one the other is instantly affected.

However, it contradicts a core principle of Einstein's Theory of Relativity which states that no information can be transmitted instantaneously or faster than the speed of light.

Since these two concepts are diametrically opposite, if one can define an experiment that shows one of these theories contradict the observable properties of entanglement while the other supports it **may** tell us which one defines why the universe is what it is.

This is because there is irrefutable experimental evidence the act of measuring the state of one of pair of photons instantaneously affect the other even though they are physically separated from each other.

As was mentioned earlier quantum physics, assumes **not only** photons but **all** particles are entangled, so that actions performed on one instantaneously affect the other, even when separated by great distances, while Einstein tells us that instantaneous or faster than light communication between to particles is impossible.

However, Einstein also told us the relative distance between two objects or points in space is defined by their relative motion and that there is no preferred reference frame by which one can define that distance.

Therefore, he tells us the distance between the observational points in a laboratory can be defined from the perspective of the photons moving at the speed of light.

Yet, his formula for length contraction also tells us the separation between the two points used to determine their entanglement from the perspective of two photons moving at the speed of light would be **zero** no matter how far apart they might be from the perspective of an observer in that laboratory.

Therefore, according to Einstein's theory all photons which are traveling at that speed are entangled no matter how far apart they may appear to be to someone who is measuring their properties. Additionally, it also tells us the information exchange between two entangle photons does not travel faster than the speed of light because from their perspective the distance between the observation points where information was measured is zero.

This tells us the entanglement of photons can be explained and predicted terms of the relativistic properties of space-time as defined by Einstein as well as by Quantum Mechanics.

(Some have suggested that if you have two photons moving in opposite directions, you can only treat one as moving at the speed of light at the same time, not both simultaneously" However that directly contradicts Relativity because it means that from the perspective of the one that is stationary the lab is moving at the speed of light away from it while the other one is moving at the speed of light in the opposite direction from the lab. However, that means the second photon is moving at twice the speed of light from the perspective of the first one. That is a direct contradiction of Relativity which tell the speed of light is the maximum attainable,

The only way to resolve this issue is to assume that from their perspective they are each moving at half speed of light with respect to the laboratory where they were entangled.

One can understand how Einstein may have viewed this by using his concept of light cones. This is because their light cones are expanding at the speed of light while the photons at their apex's are moving apart at the same speed. This tells their light cones will always intersect at the lab and be causally connected to it. However, it also tells us that each photon from the perspective of the lab will be moving in opposite directions at half the speed of light because if one draws a perpendicular from the apex of the light cone to a horizontal line through the point to where they intersect it will divide the velocity vector of each light cone in half.)

However as was mentioned earlier one of the core principals of Quantum Mechanics is that **all** entangled particles share on a quantum level one or more properties such as polarization or momentum.

This gives us a way of experimentally determining which of these two theories define why entanglement occurs because if it is found that all particles are entangled it would validate one of the core principals of Quantum Mechanics and invalidate Relativities assumption that information cannot be exchange instantaneously or faster that the speed of light while if it was found that some were not it would invalidate Quantum Mechanics because it states that **all** particle are entangled.

However, one **must use** another core principle of Quantum Mechanics defined by De Broglie that all particles are made up of waves with a wavelength defined $\lambda_{dB}= h/p$. This tells us all particles in a quantum environment have an extended volume equal to their wavelength.

Yet because Quantum Mechanics tell us **all** particles have an extended volume equal to their wavelength there will be an overlap or entanglement when observed if the distance separating them is less than the diameter or their volume as defined by its wave properties.

This tells us some particles moving slower than the speed of light **can be** entangled if the relativistic distance between the observation points from their perspective is less than their extended volume because it would mean from their perspective, they are physical connected.

This means both Relativity and Quantum Mechanics tell us that all particles should be entangled if the distance between the end points of the measurements as predicted by Relativity is less than their wavelength or volume as defined by De Broglie.

However, this gives us a **definitive** way to determine which one of these theories defines the reason for entanglement because we can precisely define the wavelength and therefore the volume of a particle by, as mentioned earlier using De Broglie formula "$\lambda_{dB} = h/p$" while one can determine, the relativistic distance between the observational points from the perspective of the particles by using Einstein formula for length contraction associated with their velocity.

If it is found entanglement **does not** occur if that distance is greater than a particle's extended volume it would invalidate the one of the core principles of Quantum Mechanics that two particles or molecules share on a quantum level one or more properties such as spin, polarization, or momentum no matter how far they are separated. If, on the other hand, it is found that entanglement **does** occur even if the relativistic separation was greater than their volume it would invalidate the core principals of Relativity that no information can be transferred faster that the speed of light.

In other words, it gives us an experimental way to **unequivocally** determine if Quantum Mechanics or Einstein's' theories define why the universe is what it is.

Article 11
Using Einstein's Theories to Explain and Predict Dark Matter.

Dark Matter is a form of matter which is thought to account for approximately 85% of the matter in the universe and the remaining is made up of visible or baryonic matter. Its presence is implied in a variety of astrophysical observations, including the gravitational affects it has on the orbits of stars in galaxies which cannot be explained by accepted theories of gravity unless more matter is present than can be seen. The reason it is called dark is because it does not appear to interact with the electromagnetic field, which means it does not absorb, reflect or emit electromagnetic radiation.

However, **we disagree that a vast majority of it cannot be explained** by the currently accepted theories because Einstein in his General Theory of Relativity defined the gravitational potential of an object in terms of the depth of a curvature in the "surface" of space-time caused by its energy density. The denser it is the greater the depth of the curvature or gravity "well" in it. For example, the Sun has a large (or deep) "gravity well" while asteroids and small moons have much shallower one.

But as Steven Weinberg, a Nobel prize winning theoretical physicist pointed out because Einstein

equation E=mc^2 tells us energy and mass is equivalent, to define the total gravitational potential of a volume of space-time one must NOT only consider that given by its baryonic matter but all forms of energy encapsulated in it.

Therefore, those who accept Einstein's theory have no choice but to assume the electromagnetic energy in a star must contribute to the gravitation potential or depth of its "gravity well".

This means, to calculate total "depth" of the curvature or "gravity well" in the "surface" of space-time created by a star one **must not only** take into consideration the quantity of energy defined by the baryonic or visible matter but also all other forms of energy in its space-time volume including electromagnetic.

However, if true it should have an observable effect on objects orbiting stars.

The reason it does it does not **appear** to is because we define the gravitational potential of a star in terms of centripetal force associated with a planets orbit and Einstein's definition of gravity.

However, using that mentioned would **not** take into account the gravitational potential of a star's electromagnetic energy because it creates an "offset" in the gravitational field of a star.

One can understand why by using an analogy of how the surface of water in a well prevents an object floating on it from sinking to the bottom. How far below its top would represent the gravitational potential of visible or baryonic matter. While that contributed by its electromagnetic energy would be represented by how far that "surface" that is offset above the bottom of the well. Therefore, the total gravitational potential of an object or star would be defined by adding that of its electromagnetic energy to the gravitational energy of it baryonic.

This means the gravitational potential experienced by an object that was **not** orbiting or gravitational bound to a star would be defined in terms of both that provided by its baryonic matter plus what Einstein tells us is provided by its electromagnetic energy because it is occupying a space-time environment that is outside of the star's gravity well not inside of it.

However, an object orbiting a star such as a planet would be on the same gravitational energy level that is defined by its baryonic mass because it would be moving on gravitation plain of space-time that was offset from the bottom of its gravity well by its electromagnetic energy content (Figure 2)

Figure 2

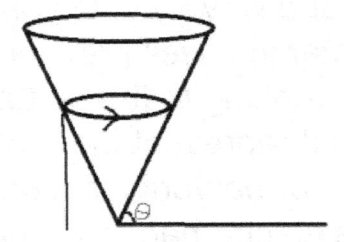

The cone represents the total depth of the gravitational well of a star's baryonic matter and electromagnetic energy while the lower circle would represent the gravitational plain where objects orbiting it would be found.

This suggest the missing dark matter component of our universe may not be related to the existence of visible baryonic matter but to the fact, as was mentioned earlier Einstein told us to define the total gravitational potential of a volume of space-time one must NOT only consider that given by its baryonic matter but all forms of energy include electromagnetic encapsulated in it.

This assumption is supported by the observation that when a star dies it collapses to a black hole composed of baryonic matter which does not contain the same quantity of electromagnetic energy as it did before the collapse. However, the orbital dynamics of objects remain the same after the collapses. This tells us that the way we define the gravitational energy of a star does not include what is contributed by its electromagnetic energy because if it did the we would observe a shift in the orbital dynamics of objects orbiting one after forming.

Some may say that the electromagnetic energy that originally kept a star from collapsing would be trapped inside a black hole. However, if that were true the star would not have collapsed.,

As was mentioned earlier the total gravitational potential of an object or star would be defined by adding that of its electromagnetic energy to the gravitational energy of it baryonic. This suggest an object that was not gravitational bound to a star would view its gravitational potential from the top of its gravity well. Therefore, it would be defined by that provided by its baryonic matter plus what Einstein tells us is provided by its electromagnetic energy provides.

This suggests the gravitational forces associated with dark matter may not related to the existence of baryonic matter but to gravitational potential Einstein associated with electromagnetic energy.

However, this also explain why its existence does not **appear** to be as prevalent in spherical galaxies as in spiral ones. This is because the electromagnetic energy opposing the gravitational collapse of a star would have a directional component parallel to the gravitational force of its baryonic matter. Therefore, the random orientation of that force vector in stars in spherical galaxies would result in it have a smaller effect on their orbital dynamics. (Figures 3 and 4).

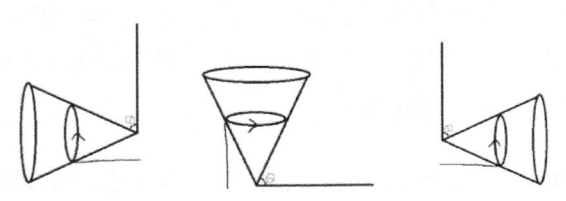

Figure 3

Figure 2 The random orientation of gravitational plains of stars in a spherical galaxy

Figure 4

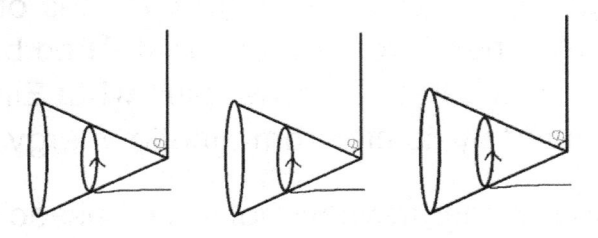

Figure4 The orientation of gravitational plains in spiral galaxies

As was mentioned earlier Steven Weinberg pointed out "Einstein showed all energy not just that which was locked up in mass is a source of gravity.

Therefore, anyone who one accepts Einstein theory has **no choice** but to accept the fact that each healthy star **must** contain at twice as much gravitational energy associated with its baryonic. This is because in a health star the its electromagnetic energy must be equal and opposite from its gravitational energy

The fact we can **unequivocally** determine how much of it is **locked** in **healthy** stars using Einstein's theories will help us determine where to look for other sources.

For example, the mass of black holes, interstellar dust and the gravitational potential of photons or electromagnetic energy in interstellar space, such as the cosmic background radiation all contribute to total the gravitation potential of the universe. Granted the energy of one unit of the CBM may not contribute much but the fact that it occupies every conner of our universe means it could make up a significant portion of dark matter.

Article 12
Understanding Gravity the Particle and Wave Properties of Electromagnetic Energy in Terms of geometry of Space-time.

In his formulation of electromagnetism Maxwell described light as a propagating electromagnetic wave created by the interaction of its electric and magnetic fields.

However, in Quantum Mechanics electric and magnetic fields are **not** propagated by a wave but the particle called a photon.

While Einstein in his General Theory of Relativity defined the forces associated with gravity in terms of a spatial displacement in the geometry of space-time caused by its energy density.

Additionally, he showed that it was directed along the one-dimensional radius of that curvature. (Figure 1)

Figure 1

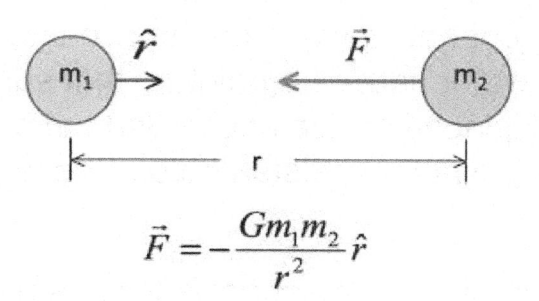

$$\vec{F} = -\frac{Gm_1 m_2}{r^2}\hat{r}$$

Therefore, one could connect the forces associated with an electromagnetic wave to those of gravity if one could define both in terms of that geometry.

As was just mentioned gravity's force vector is along the radius of one of dimensional plains of three-dimensional space. However, that does **not** mean the other two plains of three-dimensional space cannot contribute to its energy content.

It can and will be shown the electric and magnetic components of an electromagnetic wave are the result of a spatial displacement in either one of the two-dimensional plains that are perpendicular to gravity force vector.

(The reason light is polarized is because its wave properties can be propagated on one either of the two-dimensional planes that are perpendicular to each other.)

One can understand the mechanism responsible for the propagation of an electromagnet wave by using the analogy of how a wave on the two-dimensional surface of water causes a point on that surface to become displaced or rise above and below the equilibrium point that existed before the wave was present.

The science of wave mechanics tells us a force would be developed by these displacements which would result in the elevated and depressed portions of the water moving towards or becoming "attracted" to each other and the surface of the water.

Similarly, an electromagnetic wave on the "surface" of one of the two spatial dimensions that as mentioned earlier are perpendicular to the axis of gravitational forces would cause a point on that "surface" to become displaced or rise above and below the equilibrium point that existed before the wave was present.

Therefore, classical wave mechanics, if extrapolated to the properties of either one of the dimensions plains of our universe tell us a force will be developed by the differential displacements caused by an electromagnetic wave on it. This will result in its elevated and depressed portions moving towards or becoming "attracted" to each other as the wave moves through space.

This would define the causality of the attractive properties of electrical fields associated with an electromagnetic wave in terms of a force caused by the alternating displacements of a wave moving with respect to time on a "surface" of the two spatial dimensions which are perpendicular to the axis of gravitational forces.

However, it also provides a classical mechanism for understanding why similar electrical fields repel each other. This is because observations of waves show there is a direct relationship between the magnitude of a displacement in its "surface" to the magnitude of the force resisting that displacement.

Similarly, there would be a direct relationship between the magnitude of a displacement in the surface of a spatial dimension to the magnitude of the force resisting that displacement Therefore, they will repel each other because the magnitude of the force resisting the displacement will be greater than it would be for a single one.

One can also derive the magnetic component of an electromagnetic wave in terms of the horizontal force developed along the axis that is perpendicular to the displacement caused by its peaks and troughs associated with the electric fields. This would be analogous to how the perpendicular displacement of a mountain generates a horizontal force on the surface of the earth, which pulls matter horizontally towards the apex of that displacement.

This explain why the electrical and magnetic fields of an electromagnetic wave are in phase or maximum at the same time.

As was shown above the science of wave mechanics allows one to explain how electric and magnetic forces interact to form an electromagnetic wave by assuming it is moving through time on either one of the two dimensional "surfaces" of space-time that is perpendicular to the line of action of gravitational forces.

However, to understand how and why an electromagnetic wave evolves into a photon in a quantum environment one must connect its evolution to that environment.

One way of doing this is to use the fact the evolution of energy in both a quantum and space-time environment are in part defined by waves. For example, Relativity defines evolution in space-time in terms of the energy propagated by an electromagnetic wave while Quantum Mechanics defines it in terms of the mathematical evolution of the wave function. Additionally, it defines the existence of the particle properties of the wave function in terms of its interaction with an observer or its external environment.

This suggests the wave function that governs the evolution of a quantum environment may be represented by an electromagnetic wave that defines its evolution in space-time. If true one should be able to derive the existence of the particle or photonic properties of an electromagnetic wave terms its interaction with space-time.

One can accomplish this by using the science of wave mechanics and the properties of space-time as define by Einstein.

For example, the science of wave mechanics along with the fact that Relativity tells us wave energy moves continuously through space-time unless it is prevented from doing so by someone or something interacting with it. This would result in its energy being confined to three-dimensional space. The science of wave mechanics also tells us the three-dimensional "walls" of this confinement will result in its energy being reflected back on itself thereby creating a resonant or standing wave in three-dimensional space. This would cause its wave energy to be concentrated at the point in space were a particle would be found.

Additionally, wave mechanics also tells us the energy of a resonant system, such as a standing wave can only take on the discrete or quantized values associated with its fundamental or a harmonic of its fundamental frequency.

This explains why an electromagnetic wave if prevented from moving through space-time either by being observed or encountering an object is reduced or "Collapses" to a form a standing wave that would define the quantized energy Quantum Mechanics associates with a particle.

As was mentioned earlier Einstein define gravity in term of the energy density of a volume of space-time.

However as was shown above on can understand why the energy density of space is quantized using the prosperities of a space-time environment.

This tells us the quantization of gravity may **not** be a fundamental property of the universe as is suggest by Quantum Mechanics but an **emergent property** of space-time.

(Some have suggested the above explanation of Electromagnetism is incorrect because the physical orientation of its wave properties would become distorted or polarized as it passed through a gravitational field. Therefore, all light that passed through a gravitational lens would be polarized because the lateral acceleration of gravity was excluded. They feel the above explanation is falsified because this is not observed. However, because the shift in its orientation as it enters a gravitational lens would be opposite of what it would experience leaving it would cancel and therefore light traveling through one would NOT observe it to be polarized.)

Article 13
Why the Future Is What It Is.

Classical physics is causal; a complete knowledge of the past allows for the precise prediction of the future. Likewise, a complete knowledge of the future allows for the prediction of the past.

Not so in Quantum Mechanics because the probabilistic interpretation of the wavefunction tells all possible futures simultaneously exist before a measurement is made.

On the surface these probabilistic and causal definitions of the future appear to be incompatible.

However, that **may not** be the case.

As mentioned earlier, what separates the future associated with classical and relativistic physics from the probabilistic one of Quantum Mechanics is one tells us **all** of the probable outcomes of an event **exist** simultaneously while on the other hand the one defined by classical physics tells us there is only one.

However, when we role dice in a casino most do not believe there are six of them out there waiting for the dice to tell us which one we will occupy after the roll.

This is because the probability of getting a six is related to its physical interaction with properties of the table in the casino where it is rolled. In other words, the probabilities associated with a roll of dice do not define the future of the casino the casino defines the future of the dice.

Similarly, just because Quantum Mechanics defines outcome of observations in terms of probabilities would not mean all of those probable outcome's exist if they are caused by a physical interaction with the environment it occupies.

However, as was mentioned earlier the casualty of the deterministic properties of the future predicted by classical physics and the probabilistic one defined by Quantum Mechanics **may not** be as incompatible as one might think.

To show why one would have to define a shared evolutionary property of their environments. The most obvious way to do this would be to use the fact that both define their evolution in terms a wave. For example, Relativity does so it in terms of an electromagnetic one while Quantum Mechanics use the mathematical properties of the wavefunction.

This commonality suggests wavefunction which defines the evolution of a quantum system **may be** represented by an electromagnetic wave in a classical environment.

This means it could be used to understand how the interaction of quantum system with its environment creates a future outcome in terms of the classical laws of physic.

This is because classical wave mechanics tells us an electromagnetic wave moves continuously through space-time unless it is prevented from by doing so by someone or something interacting with it. This would result in its energy being confined in three-dimensional space. The science of wave mechanics also tells us the three-dimensional "walls" of this confinement will result in its energy being reflected back on itself thereby creating a resonant or standing wave in three-dimensional space. This would cause its wave energy to be concentrated at the point in space where a particle would be found. Additionally, wave mechanics also tells us the energy of a resonant system, such as a standing wave which this confinement would create can only take on the discrete or quantized values associated with its fundamental or a harmonic of its fundamental frequency.

Putting it in the vernacular of Quantum Mechanics when an electromagnetic wave is prevented from moving through space-time either by being observed or encountering an object, it "collapses" to a form a standing wave that would define the quantized energy it associates with a particle.

Additionally, as was just shown this tells us all of the probabilistic futures predicted by the wavefunction **may not** simultaneously exist if one assumes the wavefunction does **not** define the future but its environment defines the future of the wavefunction.

However, the reason the probabilistic interpretation of the future is **necessary** is because Quantum Mechanics defines the position of a particle **only** in terms of mathematical point in space. Therefore, it must define the future in terms of probabilities due to the randomness of where that point is defined with respect to a particle's center.

The reason why Relativity **appears** be deterministic is because those deviations are average out by the large number of particles in objects like the moon and planets.

This explains why the future is what it is in a quantum environment MAY be because the wavefunction does not define the future of its environment its environment defines the future of its wavefunction.

Article 14
An Alternative Explanation for the Variations in the Cosmic Background Radiation.

In the 1950s, there were two competing theories regarding the origin of the universe.

The first or the Steady State Theory was formulated by Hermann Bondi, Thomas Gold, and Fred Hoyle. It postulated that the universe was homogeneous in space and time and had remained that way forever.

The second is called the Big Bang Theory, which is based on the observations made by Edwin Hubble in 1929 that the universe was expanding.

However, a few physicists led by George Gamow a proponent of the Big Bang Theory showed an expanding universe meant it must have had its beginning in a very hot infinitely dense environment, which then expanded to generate the one we live in today.

They were able to show only radiation emitted approximately 300,000 years after its beginnings should be visible today because before that time the universe was so hot that protons and electrons existed only as free ions making the universe opaque to radiation. It was only after it cooled enough, due to is expansion to enable protons and electrons to join did it become visible. This period is referred as the age of "recombination".

Additionally, they predicted this Cosmic Background Radiation or what was left over from that period would have cooled from several thousand degrees Kelvin back when it was generated to 2.7 today.

The conflict between the Steady State and Big Bang Theory was resolved when this was discovered by Penzias and Wilson in 1965 because it showed the temperature of the universe had changed through time, which was a direct contradiction to the Steady State Model".

However, if the universe began as an expansion in an infinitely dense hot environment, one would expect the universe and the Cosmic Background Radiation (CMB) to be homogeneous because if it had been infinitely density in the beginning it must have been, by definition homogeneous. Therefore, if the universe was homogeneous when it began it should still be.

But the existence of galactic clusters and the variations in the CMB's intensity discovered by NASA's WMAP and more recently the European Space Agency Planck Satellite showed the universe was not homogeneous either now or at the time when the it was emitted.

Many proponents of the big bang model assume that these variations were caused by quantum fluctuations in the energy density of space. They define quantum fluctuations as a temporary change in the energy density of space caused by the uncertainty principle.

However, there is another possible explanation which is not based quantum fluctuations.

We still have not been able to determine if the universe will continue to expand indefinitely or if it will eventually collapse in on itself. But if it did the heat generated by its collapse could provide another explanation for the variations in the CBM if it was enough to cause protons and electrons to become ionized again. This is because the radiation pressure caused by the heat of its collapse would result in it again expanding and cooling which would enable protons and electron to again rejoin creating another age of "recombination".

This suggests the variations in it **may not** be due to a quantum phenomenon as is suggested by the Big Bang but to the randomness of the thermodynamic expansion and collapse of a previous universe.

Many proponents of the Big Bang hypothesis have **also** suggested it is the only model that can accurately predict abundance of the light-elements in today's universe. This is because both theory and observation have led astronomers to believe the mechanism responsible for creating the lighter elements (namely deuterium, helium, and lithium) occurred in the first few minutes after the Big Bang before the CBM was emitted, while the heavier elements are thought to have their origins in the interiors of stars which formed much later in the history of the universe. However, the abundance of those light elements would be dependent on rate the universe expanded and the temperature profile at each point in it.

Yet because as was mentioned earlier we are unable to observe what happened before the CBM many use the observations of their abundance in today's universe **in part** to help them define the conditions responsible for their creation. Therefore, the reason why the big bang hypothesis **can** verify the abundance of the light-elements in today's universe **may** be because it was used (in part) to determine those conditions.

However, they would not have to base their abundance on the present concentrations if one assumes it was the result, as was suggest above by the heat generated by collapse of a previous universe because one could use the science of thermodynamics to see beyond the CBN barrier.

This is because one could use the observations of the temperature and rate of expansion of our present universe to estimate when its collapse would begin and when it would begin to reexpand along with the temperature at each point in its history even before the CBM was created. This would allow one define a mechanism that is responsible for the abundance of the lighter elements and the variations in the cosmic background radiation which would be based **only** on its observable rate of expansion and **not (in part)** on the current the abundance of the lighter elements as the big bang model does.

Article 15
Integrating Gravity into Quantum Electrodynamics or QED in terms of the Field Properties of Space-time.

Quantum electrodynamics or QED is the relativistic quantum field theory of electrodynamics. It's a theoretical framework which combines classical field theory with special Relativity and the quantum mechanical properties of particles by assuming it is the result of excited states of quantum fields. It also assumes that is more fundamental than particles. However, it has not been able to derive gravity in terms of that field.

While in Relativity the exchange of energy between particles is derived terms of the evolution of its field properties caused by an electromagnetic wave and derives gravity in terms of an increase in the local energy density of space-time.

QED on the other hand uses the mathematical properties of the wavefunction **in part** to define the evolution of its environment.

This means one **may be** able to integrate gravity into QED by showing a how the interaction of both an electromagnetic wave in a Relativistic environment and mathematical one in a Quantum field is responsible for creating a quantized increase the local energy density.

This can be done by using the science of wave mechanics and the fact Relativity and QED tells us energy in the form of an electromagnetic or the mathematical properties of the wave function move continuously through their environments unless they are prevented from doing so by being observed or interacting with something. This would result in their energy being confined to a three-dimensional space. The science of wave mechanics and quantum field theory also tells us the three-dimensional "walls" of this confinement will result in its energy being reflected back on itself thereby creating a resonant or standing wave in three-dimensional space.

Additionally, wave mechanics also tells us the energy of a resonant system, such as a standing wave which this confinement would create can only take on the discrete or quantized values associated with its fundamental or a harmonic of its fundamental frequency. This would define quantum gravity in both a relativistic and quantum environment because defines how a quantized increase in the energy density of space is responsible for the creation of a particle.

Putting it in the vernacular of Quantum Mechanics when an electromagnetic wave in space-time or mathematical one in a quantum field is prevented from moving through space and time either by being observed or encountering an object it "Collapses" to a form a standing wave that would result in a quantized increase in the energy density of space.

This suggests one can use Einstein's field theories and the science of wave mechanics to define why gravity is quantized in terms of the quantized increase in the energy density caused by the creation of standing wave that was earlier shown to be responsible for a particle in both a relativistic or a quantum field.

However, we cannot observe a how the mathematical wave associated with the wave function interacts with a quantum field. This means the assumption made by QED that particles are excited states of one is **not** supported by observations.

Yet, we can observe how waves interact with the observable three-dimensional field properties of Einstein four-dimensional space-time to the explain how a quantized increase in the energy density will result in gravity also being quantized.

What we as Scientists have to decide is should we use observable properties of Einstein space-time field to construct and test hypotheses and theories on the quantization of gravity or should we base them on the unobservable properties of a QED field.

Article 16
Deriving the Probability Amplitudes of Quantum Mechanics in terms of the Dynamics of Space-time.

The evolution of Quantum environment is derived by using the probabilities associated with the wave function to define the point where a particle will most likely be found **only** after it is observed or interacts with its external environment but does not tell us why.

On the other hand, Relativity tells us the evolution of space-time is the result of electromagnetic waves transferring energy form one particle or object to another or but does not tell us a why particles such as a photon **only** appears when they encounter an object.

However, before defining why the probabilities associated with of Quantum Mechanics are the result of a dynamic property of space-time we **must** first define how and why an electromagnetic wave **only** presents itself as photon when interacting with its environment similar to how the wave function in a quantum one only becomes one when it interacts with its environment.

This can be done by using the science of wave mechanics because it and Relativity tells us an electromagnetic wave moves continuously through space-time unless it is prevented from doing so by being observed or interacting with something in its environment. This would result in its energy being confined to three-dimensional space. The science of wave mechanics also tells us the three-dimensional "walls" of this confinement will result in its energy being reflected back on itself thereby creating a resonant or standing wave in three-dimensional space. This would cause its wave energy to be concentrated at the point in space where a particle would be found.

Additionally, wave mechanics also tells us the energy of a resonant system, such as a standing wave, which this confinement would create can only take on the discrete or quantized values associated with its fundamental or a harmonic of its fundamental frequency. This means the energy of **all** particles will be quantized and have an extended volume equal to the wavelength associated with its standing wave.

The boundaries or "walls" of its confinement would be defined by its wave properties. If an electromagnetic wave is prevented from moving through space it will be reflected back on itself. However, that reflected wave still cannot move through it therefore it will be reflected back creating a standing wave. This suggest its volume is related to the wavelength of its standing wave component.

However, because Quantum Mechanics defines the evolution of its environment in term of a wavefunction and Relativity defines it in terms of an electromagnetic wave means all particles in both a quantum and relativistic environment have an extended volume related to their wavelength.

The next step in understanding why we must define the position of a particle in terms of probabilities is to look at how each define its position.

Quantum Mechanics defines it in terms of one-dimensional point while Relativity defines it in terms of one which represents the center of mass of an object or particle.

However, because both Quantum Mechanics and Relativity cannot precisely predict where that one-dimensional point is located with respect to the center of a particle's extended volume, defined earlier one **cannot** determine its exact postilion in space.

Therefore. because there is an uncertainty or randomness of where that point is with respect to a particle's volume one must use probabilities to define its position in a both a space-time and quantum environment.

This shows how one can explain why we must use probabilities to define both a quantum and classical environment.

The reason Relativity appears to be deterministic is because the error in determining the precise center of each particle is average out by the large number of them in objects like the moon and planets.

However, as the number of particles decreases the error in determining where it's center **will become more prevalent in a relativistic environment. This suggests the determination of the precise parameters of a relativistic environment may degree of probabilities when applied to a quantum one.**

Article 17
The CATASTROPHIC THEORETICAL Errors in the Big Bang Theory.

The Big Bang Theory is the leading explanation about how the universe began. At its simplest, it says the universe as we know it started with a singularity, then inflated over the next 13.8 billion years to the cosmos that we know today.

Because current instruments don't allow astronomers to peer back at the universe's birth, much of what we understand about it comes from mathematical formulas and models. Astronomers can, however, see the "echo" of the expansion through a phenomenon known as the Cosmic Background Radiation or CBR.

The idea the universe was smaller in the beginning was supported by Edwin Hubble observation in 1929 that it was expanding.

Later, a few physicists led by George Gamow a proponent of the Big Bang Model showed an expanding universe meant that it might have had its beginning in singularity or a very hot infinitely dense environment, which then expanded to create the one we live in today.

They were able to show only radiation emitted approximately 300,000 years after the beginnings of the expansion should be visible today because before that time the universe was so hot that protons and electrons existed only as free ions making the universe opaque to radiation.

Additionally, they predicted this CBR would have cooled from several thousand degrees Kelvin back when it was created to 2.7 today due to the expansion of the universe. Many thought its discovery 1965 by Penzias and Wilson provided its verification.

However, there was a problem with assuming the universe begin that way because an infinitely dense environment must have been, by definition homogeneous. Therefore, if the universe was homogeneous when it began it should still be. But the existence of galactic clusters and the variations in the intensity of the CBR discovered by European Space Agency's Planck space observatory showed the universe is not and therefore, was not homogeneous either now or at the time when it was emitted.

Many proponents of the big bang model assume that these variations in the universe were caused by quantum fluctuations in the energy density of space which are define as a temporary change in the energy of space caused by the uncertainty principle.

However, there are **catastrophic theoretical** errors in both assuming our universe originated from a singularity and the effects quantum fluctuations in the energy density of space would have on the evolution of the universe.

Einstein and **observations** of black holes tell us time moves slower as the energy density in space-time increases with respect to the center of objects and will eventually stop if it becomes great enough.

Additionally, Schwarzschild was able to use Einstein's mathematics to calculate distance from the center of one where time would stop from the perspective of an a centrally position observer. However, the energy density in around a singularity and a quantum fluctuation would be much greater than that.

This tells us because expansion cannot occur in an environment where time has stopped the universe could not have had its beginning as a singularity or a quantum fluctuation.

Therefore, because as was just mentioned Einstein's field equations and **observations** of black holes tell us there is a minimum radius the total energy content of the universe can occupy for time to move forward which **is** much larger than that of a singularity quantum fluctuation. Its expansion could not have started from one.

In other words, if the proponents of the big bang model had considered the **observable** effects energy density has on time, they would have realized that the universe could not have originated from a singularity.

Some may say that the energy density of expanding universe would not affect the rate at which time passes but they would be **wrong** because Einstein's tells us it would be related **only** to its differential energy density. In other words, he tells us the rate at which time slows and where it would stop and prevent further expansion would be determined by the differential energy density between the center of its expansion and its outer edge. Therefore, similar to a black hole the universe would have an "event horizon" which would define its minimum volume before which no expansion could occur.

However, there is a similar error behind the assumption that quantum fluctuations are responsible for variations in Cosmic Background Radiation because the energy density around their exterior by definition would great enough to cause time to stop. Therefore, quantum fluctuations could not affect the evolution of the universe or be responsible for variations in CBM because as was just mentioned evolution cannot occur in an environment where time has stopped.

Some might disagree because they say the energy in a singularity and that contained in a quantum fluctuation would be powerful enough to overcome the stopping of time predicted by Einstein mathematics. However, they would be **wrong** again because Einstein and observations tells that when the energy density reaches a certain level time will stop. It does not say that an increase beyond that point will allow it to move again.

As was mentioned earlier, current instruments don't allow astronomers to peer back at the universe's birth, much of what we understand about its origin comes from theory and mathematical formulas.

However, we may be able to define the origin of the present universe in terms of its observable properties.

We still have not been able to determine if the universe will continue to expand indefinitely or if it will eventually collapse in on itself. However, if one assumes it collapses, one could develop a mathematically model which would allow for determining when the heat generated by its collapse would cause it to re-expand. If it was found it was great enough to cause protons and electrons to exist only as free ions before the radiation pressure caused it to enter an expansion phase then another round of the Cosmic Background Radiation would be created.

This would also give one the ability to determine if the irregularities such as galactic clusters mentioned earlier in it **could** be the result of irregularities in its collapse based on observation of the irregularities that exist today.

This suggest we could define the origin of the present universe and "anisotropy" or irregularities in Cosmic Background Radiation in terms of real time observations of the present universe which would be consistent with the theoretical predictions of Einstein.

The science of Astrophysics is based almost exclusively on observations. Therefore, the question we must ask themselves is "If we have two models for the origin of the universe that predict the same outcome which one should we assume is correct?" The one that defines its origins based on the observable properties of our present universe or one that defines it in terms of the unobservable properties of a singularity.

Article 18
Should We Allow Mathematics to be the Only Definition of Reality?

One thing all theoreticians especially physicist should be aware of is the fact there are many ways to mathematically quantify what we observe but only one can define the reality behind those observations.

History has shown assuming the existence of something based primarily on the quantitative powers of mathematics and not on observations of how an environment evolves can be misleading.

For example, many thought in the Ptolemaic or geocentric system of planetary motion which used mathematics of epicycles to explain the retrograde motion of the Moon, Sun, and planets was correct.

It was not until scientific investigations were stimulated by Copernicus's publication of his heliocentric theory and Galileo's observation of the phases of the moons of Jupiter did many European scientists consider the fact it was not.

This is true even though many Greek, Indian and Muslim savants had published heliocentric hypotheses centuries before Copernicus.

However, why did it take almost thousand years for the Europeans to realize their ideas were incorrect?

One reason may have been because the math that used epicycles was able to predict their positions was within the observational tolerances of their equipment.

However, if the scientists who assumed the existence of epicycles had taken the time to observe the reality of how objects moved on earth, they would have realized there was a problem because, at least on earth, objects did **not** follow a curve path associated with epicycles.

However, because they were still able to make accurate mathematical predictions of a planet's position based on their existence, they were able to ignore those observations and suppress the more accurate Greek, Indian and Muslim ideas for almost 2000 years.

This means the heliocentric or sun center concept of planetary motion could have become the dominate paradigm long before 1610 if European scientists had not ignored the how of objects moved on earth.

Unfortunately, I do **not** believe many of today's physicists have learned that lesson.

For example, the proponents of Quantum Mechanics assume particles and wave simultaneously exist in a superposition state based solely on mathematical evolution the wave function.

However, observations of the environment we live in suggest that in "reality" particles **cannot** exist in that state.

Yet those same observations can help us to understand why they **may not**.

For example, the science of wave mechanics and Relativity tells us an electromagnetic wave moves continuously through space-time unless it is prevented from doing so by someone or something interacting with it. This would result in it being confined to three-dimensional space. The science of wave mechanics also tells us the three-dimensional "walls" of this confinement will result in its energy being reflected back on itself thereby creating a resonant or standing wave in three-dimensional space. This would cause the energy of an electromagnetic wave to be concentrated at a point in space were a particle would be found. Additionally, wave mechanics also tells us the energy of a resonant system such as a standing wave can only take on the discrete or quantized values associated with its fundamental or a harmonic of its fundamental frequency that the wave function associates with a particle.

Putting it in the vernacular of Quantum Mechanics if an electromagnetic wave is prevented from moving through space-time either by being observed or encountering an object it "Collapses" to a form a standing wave that would define the quantized energy Quantum Mechanics associates with a particle.

This means, one does not have to assume in an environment define by the wave function that particles and waves exist simultaneously because as was show above one can explain based on the observable properties of a relativistic one can show that they have the properties of both but not at the same time

The physicist Richard Feynman is credited with saying "The weird thing about Quantum Mechanics is that no one really understands it"

Scientists **especially** physicists should realize math is only a **tool** to quantify reality **not** a replacement for it.

Article 19
Karl Popper on Falsifiability.

One of the distinguishing features of many modern theories of why our universe is what it is are based on the idea that their empirical successes justify the statement of the existence of the unobservable elements.

However, Karl Popper believes there should be another requirement before an idea is considered valuable which is that it also has ability to be empirical falsified.

He presented his argument in his book "The Logic of Scientific Discovery" in which he explains how and why only those theories that are testable and falsifiable by observations add value to a scientific community because there is always a possibility the future will reveal its falsification.

He believes theories are a result of creative imagination. Therefore, the growth of scientific knowledge rests on the ability to distinguish the reality of the "real world" from one created by imagination.

Therefore, according to Karl Popper only theories, which are testable and falsifiable by observations of the "real world" add to science since they are the only ones distinguishable from an imaginary one.

He defined two different aspects of a theoretical model of the "real" world.

The first or as he calls it the "universal statement of laws" apply to the entire universe. These are more commonly called laws of nature. Newton's law of gravity would be an example of a universal statement because it can be applied throughout the universe.

The second or singular statements are defined as ones that apply only to specific events. My car stopped because it ran out of gas is an example of a singular statement because running out gas of applies only to that event.

As mentioned earlier Karl feels the value of a scientific idea should be dependent on the ability of its "statements" to be falsified and not on their ability to be proven. This is because it is possible to logically proceed from one true singular statement to falsity a universal statement even though all other singular statements may verify it.

However, determining which singular statement can result in the downfall of a scientific system is not easy as Karl points out because it is almost always possible to introduce an ad hoc or auxiliary hypotheses to successfully integrate a singular statement into almost any scientific system.

Therefore, Karl proposes that we adopt certain rules regarding how we define provability with respect to theoretical statements.

The first is all ad hoc or auxiliary theorem added to a theory to explain a specific observation must not decrease the falsifiability or testability of the theory in question. Putting it another way, its introduction must be regarded as an attempt to develop a new system which if adopted would represent a real advancement in our understanding our observable world.

An example of an acceptable theorem is Pauli's exclusion principal because it increased the precision and the testability of older quantum theories.

An example of an unacceptable one would be the contraction hypotheses proposed by Fitzgerald and Lorentz to explain the experimental findings of Michelson and Morley because it had no falsifiable consequences but only served to restore agreement between theory and experiment. Therefore, it did little to advance our understanding of the "real world".

However, advancement was achieved by Relativity because it explained and predicted observations why light is bent by gravity along with providing new consequences and testable observable effects thereby opening up new avenues to further our understanding of reality.

Karl also feels the same rules of provability should apply to the universal statement of laws or theories that apply to the entire universe.

For example, he would, as mentioned earlier consider Newton's law of gravity to be of value to the scientific community because it explained and predicted "real world" observations of planetary motion along with providing new consequences and testable physical effects thereby opening up new avenues for testing and falsification.

However, I believe he would feel that string theories have no scientific value because they hypothesized the universe is composed of one-dimensional strings whose existence is not verifiable by observations of the "real world" because by definition they are too small to be observed. Additionally, the mathematical arguments used to support their existence have no falsifiable consequences because in most cases they can be modified to restore agreement between them and experimental findings. Therefore, there is no way to verify if the mathematical worlds created in the minds of string theorists exist in the real world.

Physics is by definition an observational science. Imagination is a very important component in its advancement, however; it must be tempered with the "reality" of the observable world.

J. Black summed it up
'A nice adaptation of conditions will make almost any hypothesis agree with the phenomena.
this will please the imagination,
but does not advance our knowledge.'

Article 20
The Realty Behind the Wave Function in terms of space-time.

The Oxford Dictionary defines reality as the world or the state of things as they actually exist, as opposed to an idealistic or notional idea of them.

Currently there are two primary ways science attempts to explain and define the "reality" of our universe. The first is Quantum Mechanics or the branch of physics that defines its evolution in terms of the probabilities associated with the wave function. The other is the deterministic environment of Relativity which defines it in terms of a physical interaction between space and time.

Specifically, Relativity would define the observable positions of particles in terms of where the point defining their center of mass is located.

While Quantum Mechanics uses the mathematical interpretation of the wave function to define the most probable position of a particle when observed in terms of one-dimensional point.

Since we all live in the same universe you would expect the probabilistic approach of Quantum Mechanics to be compatible with the deterministic one of Einstein.

Unfortunately, they define two different worlds which appear to be incompatible. One defines existence in terms of the probabilities while the other defines it in terms of the deterministic properties of space and time.

However, to show why those probabilities appear to be incompatible with Relativity's determinism even though they are **not** it will be necessary to explain the evolution of quantum environment in terms of a deterministic interaction between the components of a space-time environment.

For example, when we role dice in a casino most of us realize the probability of a six appearing is related to or is caused by its physical interaction with the properties of the table and the casino where it is rolled. Putting it another way what defines the fact that six appears is **not** the probability of getting one but the interaction of the dice with the table and the casino it occupies.

This suggests to show the "reality" behind the probabilistic predictions of the wave function in terms of space-time one **must** explain how its environment evolves in terms of how the physical components of space-time interact to define a particles position.

The fact that Relativity defines its evolution in terms of the energy propagated by electromagnetic wave while Quantum Mechanics defines it in terms of the mathematical evolution of a wave function give us a starting point because it suggests evolution in both is defined in define by a wave.

One can use this commonality to define the position of a particle in terms of the deterministic properties of space-time because the science of wave mechanics along with the fact Relativity tells us an electromagnetic wave moves continuously through space-time unless it is prevented from doing so by someone observing or something interacting with it.

While in Quantum mechanics the probability of finding a particle in a specific position is defined in terms of where the wave function most likely interacts with a quantum environment. Both would result in the energy associated with the wave function and an electromagnetic wave being confined to three-dimensional space. The science of wave mechanics also tells us the three-dimensional "walls" of this confinement will result in its energy being reflected back on itself thereby creating a resonant or standing energy wave in three-dimensional space and their energy to become concentrated at the point in space where a particle would be found.

Additionally, wave mechanics also tells us the energy of a resonant system, such as a standing wave can only take on the discrete or quantized values associated with its fundamental or a harmonic of its fundamental frequency. This means a particle would occupy an extended volume of space defined by the wavelength of its standing wave.

This suggests what defines the fact a particle appears where it does **in both a quantum and** relativistic **environment** may be related to a deterministic interaction between them and the physical properties of space-time.

However, the probabilistic interpretation of the wave function is necessary to define a particle's position in Quantum Mechanics because it defines it terms of a mathematical point which **may** or **may not** be at a particle's center. Therefore, the randomness of where that point is with respect to it will result in its position, when it is observed to be randomly distributed with respect to the volume occupied by it. This means one must define its position in terms of probabilities to average the deviations that are caused by that random placement.

Yet Relativity as was mentioned earlier also defines the position of objects; like the moon, galaxies and particles in terms of a mathematical point that defines their center of mass. However, due the randomness of the thermodynamic motion of the particle components of larger masses one cannot precisely define where that point is with respect to its center.

Therefore, because similar to Quantum Mechanics Relativity cannot precisely determine where that point is located with respect the extended volume of an object it would also have to define their exact position in terms of probabilities.

However, the large number of particles in objects such as a moon or planet would result in averaging out the deviation of the position of that point making the relativistic interoperation appear to be deterministic.

This shows the reason the probabilistic environment of Quantum Mechanics is **not** incompatible with Relativity's determinism is because each **must** define the position of a particle or object in terms of a one-dimensional point which neither can precisely define with respect to their center.

As was mentioned earlier one can define reality as the world or the state of things as they actually exist, as opposed to an idealistic or notional idea of them.

Therefore, as was shown above one can physical connect the probabilistic world of Quantum Mechanics and the deterministic one of Relativity by the fact, they both define position in terms of one-dimensional point defining the center of mass or particle. Not only that but it also allows one to connect the idealistic interpretation of the of the wave function to the observable reality or the state of things as they actually exist in our three-dimensional environment.

Article 21
The Double Slit Experiment in Space-time.

Richard Feynman the father of Quantum Electrodynamics or "OED" realized the significance of Thompson's double slit experiment because he felt carefully thinking through its implications would allow one to get complete understanding of the wave particle duality of existence predicted by Quantum Mechanics.

However, as will be shown below one **can** understand it in terms of the classical properties of wave mechanics and the space-time universe defined by Einstein.

The double slit experiment is made up of a coherent source of photons illuminating a screen after passing through a thin plate with two parallel slits cut in it. Their wave properties cause them to interfere after passing through both slits, creating an interference pattern of bright and dark bands on the screen. However, at the screen, the light is always found to be absorbed as discrete particles, called photons.

When only one slit is open, the pattern on the screen is a diffraction pattern however, when both slits are open, the pattern is similar but with much more detailed. These facts were elucidated by Thomas Young in a paper entitled "Experiments and Calculations Relative to Physical Optics," published in 1803 wrote "To a very high degree of success, these results could be explained by the method of Huygens–Fresnel principle that is based on the hypothesis that light consists of waves propagated through some medium.

However, discovery of the photoelectric effect made it necessary to go beyond classical physics and take the quantum nature of light into account because it showed that it was composed of particles called photons.

The most baffling part of this experiment comes when only one photon at a time impacts a barrier with two opened slits because an interference pattern forms which is similar to what it was when multiple photons were impacting the barrier. This is a clear implication the particle called a photon has a wave component, which simultaneously passes through both slits and interferes with itself. (The experiment works with electrons, atoms, and even some molecules too.)"

Additionally, the diffraction pattern changes when a detector measures which slit a photon passes through

Many believe the importance of this experiment is that it demonstrates both the duality of the wave and particle properties of photons and the concepts of superposition and quantum interference.

Yet, one can understand this experiment in terms of the classical properties of waves and Relativity because they tell us an electromagnetic wave moves continuously through space-time unless it is prevented from doing so by someone observing or something interacting with it. This would result in its energy being confined in three-dimensional space. The science of wave mechanics also tells us the three-dimensional "walls" of this confinement will result in its energy being reflected back on itself thereby creating a resonant standing wave in three-dimensional space. This would cause its energy to be concentrated at the point in space where a particle would be found. Additionally, wave mechanics also tells us the energy of a resonant system, such as a standing wave which this confinement would create can only take on the discrete or quantized values associated with its fundamental or a harmonic of its fundamental frequency.

Additionally, it also tells us a particle would have an extended volume equal to the wavelength associated with its standing wave.

(Note the boundaries or "walls" of its confinement would be defined by its wave properties. If an electromagnetic wave is prevented from moving through space it will be reflected back on itself. However, that reflected wave still cannot move through space therefore it will be reflected back creating a standing wave. Putting it another way the wave itself defines its boundaries because if it cannot move though space it MUST STAND in place in the form of a standing wave.)

Putting it in the vernacular of Quantum Mechanics when an electromagnetic wave is prevented from moving through space-time either by being observed or encountering an object its "Collapses" to a form a standing wave that would define the quantized energy Quantum Mechanics associates with a particle.

This explains why the interference pattern remains when a photon encounters the barrier with both slits open or "the most baffling part of this experiment" is because, as mentioned earlier it is made up of an electromagnetic wave, therefore it occupies an extended volume which is directly related to its wavelength.

This means a portion of its energy could simultaneously pass through both slits, if the diameter of its volume exceeds the separation of the slits and recombine on the other side to generate an interference pattern.

However, as was mentioned earlier if its energy is prevented from moving through space by contacting the screen it will be confined to three-dimensional space causing it to be concentrated in a standing wave that as mentioned earlier would define the energy of the photon that impacted the screen. Since the energy of a photon would be defined by the frequency of its standing wave it would have the same properties as the ones that originally passed through the slits

It also is observed if two slits are open but a detector is added to determine which one a photon has passed through, the interference pattern associated with it yields two simple patterns, one from each slit, without interference.

However, the energy of the standing wave which was earlier shown to define the quantum properties of a photon is dependent on its frequency. Therefore, if the frequency of one of the standing waves was altered by its being detected as it passed through one of the slits it would have a different energy content and therefore a different frequence than the one that was not detected. This means the interference pattern created by their standing wave properties would form a uniquely different one from the one that was not detected and would not interact with it.

This provides an experimental way of determining if the results of the Thompson's double slit experiment could be explained in terms of the physical properties of standing wave which earlier defined the quantum properties of the photon. This is because one could determine how the frequency of one was altered by it being detected and see if the shape of the interference patten that resulted from that could explain the shape of the pattern that appears on the screen of the double slit experiment.

Article 22
Why the Laws of Physics do not Break Down in a Black Hole?

Many believe a singularity exists at the center of a black hole. This belief often taken as proof the Theory of General Relativity has broken down, which is perhaps not unexpected as it occurs in conditions where quantum effects should become important.

However, observations and Einstein's prediction confirm the strength of the gravitational field at the event horizon of one will cause time to **stop** for all observers. The question is, "How can matter move beyond it if time has stopped with respect to it?" Since motion is define as the change in an objects position over time the General Theory of Relativity does not break down because it tells us matter cannot free fall after passing the event horizon of one.

Even so, in **1939 Robert** Oppenheimer and Snyder using Einstein's theories described how infalling matter would be in free fall after passing through one.

This is the bases for the conclusion that a singularity is found at the center of black hole.

However, as will be shown that is not consistent with **Einstein's theories because he told us time is dilated** by a gravitational field and essentially stops at the event horizon of one. This means according to the laws of physics developed by him a singularity cannot form in one because as was mentioned earlier if time has stop motion cannot occur because as was mentioned earlier it is defined as change in an objects position with respect to time. Therefore, matter cannot move past the event horizon from the perspective of an **external** observer. This means, the laws as defined by him are not violated with respect to an observer in that reference frame.

Yet, Einstein developed his Theory of Relativity based on the equivalence of all inertial reference frames which he defined as ones that move freely under their own inertia because they are not pushed by a force.

Yet this means one must consider the **center** of a black hole as one.

(Einstein would have considered this point an inertial reference frame with respect to its gravitational field because the field on one side will be offset by the one on the other side. Therefore, he would have considered it to be one because an observer at its center would not be "pushed or pulled and would move onward with the same motion as the gravitational field of the black hole.)

However, some have suggested if the collapse was uneven, it should not be considered one because its center would be "pushed or pulled" due to the differential gravitational force cause by its collapse. But the laws governing time dilation in Einstein's theory tell us time would move slower for those objects as they get closer to the event horizon allowing the ones further away to catch up. This tells us matter at every point where it is infalling will be at the event horizon at the exact same time and its center will not experience any pushing or pulling. Therefore, it could be considered an inertial reference frame.)

However as was mentioned earlier Einstein told us time is dilated by the relative strength of a gravitational field. Therefore, the time dilation will increase as it approaches the event horizon of a black hole relative to an observer at its **center** until it becomes frozen at its critical circumference.

Therefore, because motion cannot occur in an environment where time has stopped the laws of physics as defined by Einstein do not break down for an observer who is at the center of a black hole.

Many physicists also assume the mass of a star implodes when it reaches the critical circumference. Therefore, an observer on its surface will be in free fall with respect to its gravitational field when as it passes through its critical circumference.

This indicates an observer who on its **surface**, according to Einstein's theories could also be considered in an inertial reference frame because he is in free fall will not experience its gravitational forces.

However, according to Einstein's theory, as an object nears its critical circumference an observer who is freefalling on its surface will perceive the differential magnitude of the gravitational field relative to an observer who is in an external reference frame or is at its center to be increasing.

Therefore, he or she will perceive time in those reference frames that are not freefalling towards it slowing to a crawl as it approaches the critical circumference. The closer they get the slower time moves with respect to all external reference frames including the one that exists at its center and stops respect to them before when it reaches it.

However, the contraction of a star's surface must be measured with respect to the external reference frames in which it is contracting. But as was mentioned earlier Einstein's theories indicate time in its external environment or the center of a black hole it was freefalling into it would become infinitely dilated or stops when it reaches its critical circumference.

However, as was mentioned earlier the movement of matter towards one must be measured with respect to all reference frames.

Therefore, because motion cannot occur in an environment where time has stopped the laws of physics as defined by Einstein do not break down for an observer who is free falling into a black hole.

Yet, as was just shown Einstein's theories indicate time on the event horizon stops when viewed all reference frames.

Therefore, because the Laws of Relativistic physics tell us time stops or becomes frozen at the event horizon with respect to all observers, matter cannot move beyond it.

However, it also tells us, the laws of Relativistic physics are not violated in black hole because the time dilation associated with its gravitational field, the collapse of matter cannot proceed beyond its event horizon to form a singularity.

Article 23
The Effect Gravity has on the geometry of Space-time Inside a Black Hole.

In an earlier article (Article 22 "Do the laws of physics break down in a black hole?" (Page 116) we described what happens to matter as it falls into a black hole and why a singularity cannot form at its center with respect to time as define by Einstein Theory of Special Relativity.

However, now we would like to explain why one cannot form in terms of the effects gravity has on the geometry of a space-time.

The German physicist Karl Schwarzschild was the first to predict the existence of a black hole when in 1915, he found a solution to Einstein's field equations which predicted the existence of a spherical curvature in space-time which matter would take an infinite amount to time to cross. The observations of black holes confirmed this.

Additionally, he determined it would occur where the strength of its gravitational field was strong enough to create a spherical curvature or event horizon in the geometry of space-time

Later in 1939 Robert Oppenheimer and Snyder suggested that matter after passing though one would continue to "free fall" towards its center forming a singularity where its entire mass is concentrated in a one-dimensional point.

As mentioned earlier, Einstein's field equations which were used to define where the event horizon occurs in a black hole did so in terms of where the strength of its gravitational field created a spherical curvature in space-time.

However, the curvature at every point along the radius of a black hole where the gravitational field is strong enough with respect to its center will also have a spherical curvature.

(This is supported by the observation that the potential energy of a gravitational field maintains its spherical curvature below its surface.)

Therefore, according to Einstein matter **could not** free fall towards the center of a black hole because it would take and infinite amount of time to pass through each individual spherical layers of space-time in a black hole.

Therefore, even if an object did pass through the event horizon of one it **could not** freefall towards its center because according to Karl Schwarzschild and observations it would take an infinite amount of time to pass through each individual spherical layer of space-time in a black hole.

So, if a singularly is not at the center of a black hole what is?

We know the densest form of observable matter is found in a neutron star where the gravitational forces are strong enough to overcome the forces keeping electrons protons and neutron apart.

However, their gravitational potential is not large enough to create the spherical curvature in space-time associated with the event horizon or a black hole.

Observations also tell us a neutron star is capable of becoming a black hole if it absorbs enough mass and energy to form one. However, that does not mean that its neutron core collapses or freefalls to a singularity.

This is because as it absorbs matter its gravitation force increases to the point where it will create a spherical curvature in space-time that defines a black hole.

However, Einstein's equations tell us at every point below the radius where the gravitational field is strong enough will have the same spherical curvature.

Therefore, because as was show above matter does not free fall into the event horizon of a black hole, we should NOT assume that it will do so after passing through the ones.

This suggests the center of a black hole may NOT be made up of matter that has imploded to singularity but instead is made up of the core of a neutron star and any additional matter will be internally trapped in successive layers of the spherical geometry of space-time that Einstein's equations tell us **must** exist below the event horizon of a black hole.

Some have suggested the geodesic equations that generalizes the notion of a "straight line" to curved spacetime would cross in a black hole thereby contradicting the above explanation.

However, Einstein tells us, when a particle enters a black hole, a new and different world line is created by the concentric circular geodesic it would form in space-time with respect to one that enter before it. This means because of their concentric orientation the individual world lines of each particle do NOT cross each other and therefore cannot interact. This suggest the gravitational potential of a black hole is stored similar how a dam stores the potential energy of water.

 A dam prevents water from falling to its lowest energy level. Similarly, because the individual concentric circular geodesic in each particle that enters a black hole cannot interact, they would be prevented from falling to their lowest gravitational potential.

Article 24
Why the graviton is
so hard to detect in terms
of space-time.

Quantum Mechanics assumes the mathematical evolution of the wavefunction is responsible for quantization of ALL mass and energy. Additionally, it assumes it exists in a superposition of several eigenstates and reduces or collapses to a particle **only** when it interacts with its environment or an observer.

Therefore, many feel detecting gravitons, the hypothetical quanta of gravity, would prove gravity is quantized. The problem is that gravity is extraordinarily weak and for that reason, detecting them is extremely difficult.

However, Einstein in his General Theory of Relativity defined gravity in terms of the energy density of space. Therefore, one way of defining quantum gravity would be to show how and why it is quantized in terms of his theory in a manner that is consistent with the mathematical foundations of Quantum Mechanics.

The fact gravitational waves have been observed suggests it has properties similar to other energy waves, such as electromagnetic **with one very**

important difference: they do **not** interact with its environment or an observer in the same way. For example, unlike electromagnetic waves they pass though objects such as planets as if they were not there.

This suggests one reason why a graviton is so hard to detect while the photon or quantum of electromagnetic energy MAY NOT be related to its weakness but to how it interacts with its environment.

But before we can understand why in terms of space-time, we need to establish a connection between the evolution of the wavefunction and electromagnetic waves in a space-time environment.

This can be accomplished because in Relativity evolution of a space-time environment is defined by an electromagnetic wave while, as was mentioned earlier the mathematics of the wave function defines how a Quantum environment evolves to create a particle.

This commonality suggests the wave function MAY BE a mathematical representation of an electromagnetic wave in space-time. However, if this is true one should be able to derive the reason that is consistent with the mathematical foundations of Quantum Mechanics.

This can be done by using the science of wave mechanics and the fact that Relativity tells us an electromagnetic wave moves continuously through space-time unless it is prevented from doing so by someone or something interacting with it. This would result in it being confined to three-dimensional space. The science of wave mechanics also tells us the three-dimensional "walls" of this confinement will result in its energy being reflected back on itself thereby creating a resonant or standing wave in three-dimensional space. This would cause its energy to be concentrated at the point in space were a particle would be found. Additionally, wave mechanics also tells us the energy of a resonant system such as a standing wave can only take on the discrete or quantized values associated with its fundamental or a harmonic of its fundamental frequency.

(The boundaries or "walls" of its confinement would be defined by its wave properties. If an electromagnetic wave is prevented from moving through space it will be reflected back on itself. However, that reflected wave still cannot move through space therefore, it will be reflected back creating a resonate standing wave.)

However, as was mentioned earlier gravitational waves are different because unlike other forms of energy waves which are effectively stopped when their interact with their environment, they pass through it virtually unaffected. Therefore, their energy will not be confined to three-dimensional space and quantized as is the case as other energy waves.

For example, gravity waves have only been observed when they squeeze and stretch space. However, that observation does not result in an exchange of energy between it and the observer.

However, Quantum Mechanics assumes the wave function reduces to a quantized unit of energy **only** when it is observed or interacts with its environment.

This suggests the reason why a graviton is so hard to detect MAY NOT be because it is weak but MAY be related to how we are trying to observe it.

Putting it another way Quantum Mechanics tells us just watching a gravitational wave pass by will not produce a graviton.

Article 25
A Possible Solution to the Problems of Quantum Computing.

There are two primary ways Quantum computers are different from conventional ones. The first is it uses qubits which can exist in a superposition of multiple states to process information instead of binary bits of zeros or ones.

For example, in a classical computer two bits can hold one of four values at any time: "00," "10." "01," and "11." Therefore, at 2 billion operations per second, a standard 64-bit computer would take around 400 years to cycle through all its possible values. Qubits, on the other hand, can hold a zero, a one, or any proportion of both zero and one at the same time. An array of qubits can use superposition to instantly represent all 2^64 or 18,446,744,073,709,551,616 possible values at once, allowing a quantum computer to solve problems that are practically impossible for standard computers.

The second is entanglement which defines the physical relationship between two or more qubits in which one seems to instantly know what happens to another, even when they are a large distance apart. Therefore, entangled qubits become a system with a single quantum state. If you measure one qubit (i.e., collapse its superposition to a single state), you will have the same impact on the other qubits in the system.

According to research entanglement is necessary for a quantum algorithm to offer an exponential speed-up over classical computations because it allows for instantly changing the state of an entangled pair.

The fact that photons are entangled over long distances has been experimental proven beyond a shadow of a doubt.

However, one must be careful not to make **hasty** assumptions as to why because knowing more about the physical properties of the operating environment of a device can greatly streamline the design of everything from the components in modern computers to the those in a quantum one.

Therefore, one must be careful not to the extrapolate **unique** properties of a photon like the fact that they are the only particle that has been experimentally proven to be entangled at interstellar distances and that it is the only one that moves at the speed of light to other ones that might be used to create a qubit.

This is because Einstein in Special Relativity showed photons have properties that are not shared with any other particle and tells us the reason they **are** entangled **may be** different from those given by Quantum Mechanics.

He showed, due to relativistic length contraction the observed distance between the measurement of the end points of an observation would be shorter from the perspective of objects or particles in motion than it would be from the perspective of the observer. Additionally, his math defining that contraction tells us that distance will be zero for any particle moving at the speed of light.

However, he also told us that due to the relativistic properties space and time there is no preferred reference frame by which one can measure distance.

Therefore, one would be justified in measuring the distance between the end points of an observation from the perspective of photons as well as from the laboratory environment where they are being observed.

However, due to the relativistic shortening of length **all** photons which are moving at the speed of light will be entangled because from their perspective, the distance they have traveled with respect to will be **zero** no matter where they are.

As was mentioned earlier many believe Quantum Mechanics provide the only reason why entanglement occurs.

However, as was show above Einstein provided an alternative explanation as to why with respect to photons, which is just a valid as the one provided by Quantum Mechanics.

Since as was mentioned earlier, knowing which one is responsible will give engineers a better understanding the strengths and limitations of entanglement and will hopefully allow them to design systems that will take better advantage of it.

However, it does not mean a quantum computer cannot be made even if entanglement is a relativistic property of the universe because the physical properties of all particles such as spin can overlap or be entangled. This is because the de Broglie wavelength which is another concept used by Quantum Mechanics defines the wavelength associated with a particle in terms of its momentum and mass. This tells us that all particles in a qubit will occupy an extended volume of space associated with that wavelength which means all particles will be entangled if the distance between them is physically less than their de Broglie wavelength. Therefore, they will be entangled if the distance is less than that.

(This also provides an experimental way to **unambiguously** determine if entanglement is a result of a relativistic or quantum property of space. This is because if it was found entanglement ceased when the relativistic distance between the end points of an observation, when viewed from the perspective of a particle moving slower than the speed of light with respect to another was greater than its De Broglie wavelength, it would have a tendency to verify the conclusion that it is relativistic property of space-time. If not, it would indicate that it **must be** the result of its quantum properties.)

This suggests designers **may be** more successful in creating a quantum computer if they chose particles with the longest De Broglie wavelength for their Qubits and position them as closely as possible to increase the overlap of their wave properties.

Article 26
Could the Energy Density of a Collapsing Universe Be Responsible the beginning of our universe?

In article 26 Sir Roger Penrose developed a theory known as "Conformal Cyclic Cosmology" in which he postulated the universe has gone through infinite cycles. He suggested each cycle starts out from a singularity in a Black hole before expanding and generating clumps of matter, which eventually gets sucked up by super massive black holes, which over the very long term disappear by continuously emitting Hawking radiation.

But there is another way in which black holes could have contributed to its expansion based on General Relativity that does **not** have its origins in a singularity or Hawking radiation but in rapid release of energy in black holes caused by the increasing energy density of a collapsing universe.

Some will probably say that it is crazy to assume they could cause its rapid expansion however we think it is crazier to assume that it began as a one-dimensional point called a singularity as is suggested by many proponents of the Big Bang model of our universe's organ.

Cosmologists have not yet determined if the universe will keep on expanding or enter a contraction phase.

However, if it does its energy density and temperature would increase due to its matter and energy being confined to a smaller volume.

One could use that fact to define how a black hole would contribute to its expansion This is because Einstein defined gravity in terms of the differential energy density of space. This means the universe's the energy density increase due to its collapse would result in the event horizon of a black hole to expand outward because the energy differential between it and the surrounding space decreases. This would result in releasing some of its stored energy.

Granted the energy released by the expansion of a single one would have a small effect on the universe.

However, the **cascading** release of energy due to the positive feedback loop created by a large number over a short period of time **would** result in an **exponential** increase in its temperature and its expansion rate.

The science of thermodynamics defines how the universe's energy density would increase as it collapses. This means one could use observations of the present one to estimate if energy density generated by the momentum of its collapse would become great enough to cause the event horizon of a black hole expand and release its stored energy. Additionally, it would allow one to use those same observations to estimate the temperature at which expansion began and the rate at which it took place.

One advantage of this conjecture is it defines a mechanism for the origins of our current universe in terms of its currently observable properties. This is because, one can, through observations estimate the total energy content and number of the black holes in the universe at the time its collapse began based on how many presently exist and how many will be created when all of the stars use up their fuel and collapse to one. This would **not only** allow one to estimate the rate of its reexpansion but when it would occur based on their numbers and rate at which their energy would have been released by the process outlined above.

One of the **core** principals of relativity is that energy cannot be propagated faster than the speed of light.

This means if the universe did begin as a dissociation of black's holes its temperature would increase exponentially because its expansion rate could not faster than the speed of light.

This may provide a solution to the horizon problem because according to relativity; the universe's boundaries could not expand faster than the speed of light its components would be trapped in a relativity small volume giving them enough time to interact with each other as it expanded.

This also means it would not be necessary to assume each cycle starts out from the unobservable prosperities of a singularity before expanding as the Big Bang model assumes because as was show above the laws of thermodynamic tell us it could have begun by an exponential release of energy stored in a large number of black holes which are observable.

To determine if this idea is creditable, one must **first** determine if an increase in the energy density of the universe resulting in a decrease in the surrounding space and a black hole and would cause the event horizon of a one to expand. Using that information, one **may** be able to calculate the temperature at which its expansion would have begun. and how rapidly it would cascade though all of the remaining black holes in the universe. Then using that information, one **may** be able to derive the rate of its expansion at the time it began and every point in its history based on observations of the present universe.

Yet if above hypostasis is true, it would mean its **rate** of expansion which was **in part** used to determine the concentration of the lighter elements would be different from that predicted by the currently accepted

Big Bang or Sir Roger Penrose Conformal Cyclic Cosmology.

Additionally, it provides another way to explain the irregulates in the CBM (Cosmic Background Radiation) because as was mentioned earlier it suggests that due to the fact that it could not expand faster than the speed of light there would be enough time for **most** of the irregularities cause by an uneven collapse of the previous universe to smoothed out while leaving the ones that have been observed in the cosmic background radiation

The above model would allow us to define our universe's expansion based on the mathematical analysis or computer simulations from its observable properties instead of the unobservable properties of a singularity or Hawking radiation as is suggest by the Cyclic Cosmological model defined above.

Article 27
Einstein's Block Universe
Fact or Fiction?

According to Einstein we live in a universe made up of fixed blocks of space-time while assuming the change measured by time is a result of movement through each successive block. However, it is also possible it is not the result of us moving **through** them but **in** them.

But before we can continue, we must first define what time is.

Some define it only in the abstract saying it is an invention of the human consciousness that gives us a sense of order, a before and after so to speak. While many physicists define it in terms of the properties of Einstein's space-time universe.

However, even thorough physicists define it in terms of the physical properties of a space-time dimension they also use it to give them a sense or measure of the order for change.

As was mentioned earlier Einstein in his Block Universe defined the passage of time in terms of our movement through successive fixed blocks of space-time.

However, this means your birth death and every other moment of your life is out there in space-time waiting for you to arrive.

This also suggests that free will does not exist because your future is etched in a "block" of it waiting for you to move through it and there is nothing you can do to change it.

Yet, he provided another way to explain the past, present and future when he derives the casualty of change in terms of a dynamic interaction between energy and space. This is because it gives us a way to define how and why change occurs in terms of us moving **in** space instead of moving through static ridged blocks of it.

One can understand why by using an example of two dots on the surface of a balloon. The surface of the balloon will represent the "surface" of three-dimensional space and the environment outside of it will represent the time dimension.

If one pushes down on its surface, it will cause the two dots to move. But if the pressure on the balloon is released the dots would return to their original position.

Putting it another way the dynamic interaction of its surface with the pressure or energy applied to it is responsible for the change in position of the dots.

However, if one accepts the definition of time given earlier that it is a measure of the sequential ordering of events one would know that it did not travel back in time because the return to its original position is the next event in a sequence of events that defined its position.

As was mentioned earlier Einstein derived the casualty of change in terms of a dynamic interaction between energy and space. Therefore, one could define change in terms of that interaction. This suggests the changes that earlier defined time are the result of moving in a dynamic space/energy environment instead of moving through rigid blocks of it.

However, if physicists accept the definition given above that time is a measure of when an event occurred in relation to arbitrary reference point attached to the sequence of events one can understand why it is irreversible. This is because if one chooses a reference point to define when an event occurred the time required for the next event occur in that sequence such as returning to its starting point must be added to it.

However, it also tells our future is not predetermined because we have the ability to decide how we what to use energy to influence it.

Article 28
Quantum Tunneling in Space-time.

Most assume Quantum tunneling is a quantum mechanical phenomenon where a particle can propagate through a potential barrier that it should not be able to.

Many assume the only explanation for the fact that a particle such as a proton or electron can pass through a potential energy barrier, that, according to classical mechanics, does not have sufficient energy to do so is defined by quantum mechanics. (Figure 5)

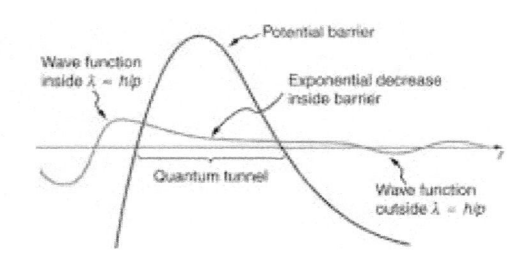

Figure 5 Diagram of Quantum tunneling

However, observations of our space-time environment suggest otherwise.

Quantum theory defines where a particle will be observed in terms of the probabilities derived from the wave function.

Therefore, to understand how quantum tunneling maybe related to a property of space-**time** environment, we should first attempt to define a physical connection between it and a quantum one.

This can be accomplished because relativity defines the evolution of its environment terms of an electromagnetic wave while, the wave function defines how a quantum environment evolves to the point where it is observed.

This commonality suggests the wave function in a quantum one could be represented by an energy wave in space-time one.

One can connect them because the science of wave mechanics and Relativity tells us an electromagnetic wave moves continuously through space-time unless it is prevented from doing so by someone or something interacting with it. This would result in it being confined to three-dimensional space. The science of wave mechanics also tells us the three-dimensional "walls" of this confinement will result in its energy being reflected back on itself thereby creating a resonant or standing wave in three-dimensional space. This would cause its energy to be concentrated at the point in space were a particle would be found.

Additionally, wave mechanics also tells us the energy of a resonant system such as a standing wave can only take on the discrete or quantized values associated with its fundamental or a harmonic of its fundamental frequency that the wave function associates with a particle.

This establishes a physical connection between the wave function in a quantum environment and an electromagnetic wave in a space-time one because it defines how and why when an energy wave interacts with an observer or its environment in space-time is it creates a standing wave which earlier define the quantized unit of energy called a particle.

As was mentioned earlier many believe the ability of a particle to penetrate through a potential energy barrier that is higher in energy than it should can only be explain by assuming it is a quantum mechanical phenomenon.

However, one can use the science of wave mechanics and observations to show that **may not** be true.

Classical Wave mechanics and observations tell us when two waves constructively interfere, they will produce one whose amplitude is greater than the original one. This means, their interference **may** create one large enough to allow some of its energy to spill over a potential energy barrier that is higher than that associated with the original wave.

Similarly, when wave mechanics is applied to a particle's standing wave component in a space-time environment it tells us that if two of them constructively interfere, they may produce one whose energy **may** be great enough to penetrate a potential barrier that would be impossible for one of the origin waves to penetrate.

Some have suggested that the wave properties of particles **cannot** interfere to create one with enough energy to go through a barrier with more energy than they have. However, interference patten observed in Thompsons double slit experiment (Article 21 page 107) tells us they can. This define a classical reason how their wave properties **could** interact to form one that can "spill" over a potential energy barrier that they should not be able to.

Additionally wave mechanics also tells us the energy associated with a resonant system such as the standing wave which earlier defined the quantum properties of a particle is primarily dependent on its frequency. Therefore, if an electromagnetic wave has an energy amplitude twice the value of it resonant standing wave it would create two particles not one. This suggest if interference of the wave component of a particle result in it having a potential energy amplitude greater than a barrier it could override it forming another a particle with a standing wave of the same frequency on the other side of it and any remaining energy being reflected from the barrier.

This shows how the classical property of a space-time environment can explain how the wave component of a particle can tunnel "through" an energy barrier they should not be able to if ones assumes that it is a result of the interaction of a particle's wave component.

Article 29
A Classical Reason why energy is quantized in terms of the observable properties of our universe.

Quantum Mechanics assumes the quantization of energy is a mathematical property of the wave function. However, Classical Wave Mechanics provides another explanation based on the observation that a system which is oscillating at its natural or a harmonic of resonant frequency is one the most efficient ways to store and transfer energy between different storage modes. This suggest the reason atoms store energy in quantized units of energy is because the most efficient way to store their energy is in resonate systems **not** just because Quantum mechanics tell us they do.

One of the core principals of Quantum Mechanics is that the energy is propagated through a quantum environment by the mathematical properties of the wave function.

Therefore, to verify the reason the quantization of energy in an atom **may not** be because Quantum Mechanics tell us it is but a classical one, we must connect the wave properties of a quantum environment to the classically observable ones of our universe.

One can accomplish this by using the fact that both Quantum and classical mechanics tell us the results of an interaction of an electromagnetic wave or the mathematical properties of the wave function defines the evolution of their respective an environment.

This commonality suggests the wave function could be a mathematical representation of an electromagnetic wave in space-time.

For example, the science of wave mechanics tells us the energy of an electromagnetic wave would move continuously through space-time unless it is prevented from doing so by being observed or something interacting with it. This would result in it being confined to volume of three-dimensional space. The science of wave mechanics also tells us the three-dimensional "walls" of this confinement will result in its energy being reflected back on itself thereby creating a resonant or standing wave in three-dimensional space.

Additionally, wave mechanics also tells us the energy of a resonant system such as a standing wave can only take on the discrete or quantized values associated with its fundamental or a harmonic of its fundamental frequency.

This shows how one can explain and predict the evolution of a quantum environment **based on observations** the observable properties of our environment.

However, it also provides a Classical explanation for the wave particle duality of existence which is one of the core principles Quantum Mechanics because it explains why, if the wave properties of energy is prevented from moving through space either by being observed or encountering an object it, it will present itself as a particle in both a space-time or quantum environment

Science of wave mechanics also tells us the wave energy associated with an electron would move continuously in the space around the nucleus it is bound to. However, as mentioned earlier a system which is oscillating at its natural or harmonic of its resonant wavelength is one the most efficient ways to store energy. Therefore, the most efficient way to store it would be in a wave moving in a path where the circumference is equal to the wavelength or a harmonic of it resonate system.

This tell us the energy of the electron orbital in an atom **may not** be quantized just because Quantum Mechanics say they are but because the most efficient way to store their energy is in a quantized resonant system.

Therefore, if an electromagnetic wave interacted with an atom orbital it **would** do so by exchanging energy in quantized units equivalent to the energy difference between the resonant standing waves surrounding the nucleus.

This shows how one can use the observable properties of our universe and classical wave mechanics to define why energy is quantized in an atom. This also suggest the quantization of the atomic orbitals may be related to property of a classical environment and not the mathematical properties of the wave function.

Both Quantum Mechanics and as was shown above classical wave mechanics gives valid reasons why for the quantization of energy in an atom. Quantum Mechanics assumes they do not because their energy is quantized based only on the assumption it is.

Yet, as was show above classical wave mechanics gives another reason which is just as valid in terms of the observable properties of standing waves

Physics is a science based on observation. Therefore, if two ideas give the same result one should give more creditability to the one which can be verified observationally instead of one that cannot.

(Note The reason why an electron does not fall into the nucleus is presented in Article 39 "Defining the strong and weak nuclear forces in terms of geometry of space-time". (page 187) in terms of an interaction between the strong and weak nuclear forces.)

Article 30
Quantum Superpositioning Explained in Terms of Space-time.

Classical physics and relativity assume that things cannot simultaneously exist in two different states at the same time.

Not so in Quantum Physics because it assumes it is made up of particles and waves which are superpositioned or simultaneously exist as a strange combination of both and only becomes a particle when observed or interacts with its environment.

However, to explain superpositioning in terms of space-time one must show how and why their wave and particle properties become intertwined in that environment.

For example, the science of wave mechanics and Relativity tell us an electromagnetic wave moves continuously through space-time unless it is prevented from doing so by being observed or something interacting with it. This would result in its energy being confined in three-dimensional space. The science of wave mechanics also tells us the three-dimensional "walls" of this confinement would result in its energy being reflected back on itself thereby creating a resonant or standing wave in three-dimensional space. This would cause its wave energy to be concentrated at the point in space where a particle would be found.

Additionally, wave mechanics also tells us the energy of a resonant system, such as a standing wave which this confinement would create can only take on the discrete or quantized values associated with its fundamental or a harmonic of its fundamental frequency. This explains the quantized or particle properties of a quantum existence in terms of the physical properties of the space-time universe define by Einstein.

Putting it in the vernacular of Quantum Mechanics if an electromagnetic wave is prevented from moving through space either by being observed or interacting with the external world it creates a standing wave that would define the quantized energy Quantum Mechanics associates with a particle.

This suggests the assumption a quantum environment is made up of a superposition or simultaneous existence of both at waves and particles **may** not be correct. Because as was shown above classical physics can be used to explain all of the observed properties of one in terms it being made up one or the other but not both at the same time.

Article 31
Why the Arrow of Time
is Irreversible.

Before we explain why the arrow of time is irreversible, we should define what time is.

Some define it only in the abstract saying it is an invention of the human consciousness that gives us a sense of order, a before and after so to speak. While many physicists define it in terms of the physical properties of a space-time dimension.

However, even thorough physicists define it in those terms they also use it to give them a sense of order for change.

This definition suggests a unit of time may be measure of sequential ordering of change in space-time similar to how a unit of length is measure of the position of an object in space because similar to time, length is perceived only as measurement of where in relation to arbitrary reference point in space an object is located.

However, Einstein defined the energy required for a change in terms of a dynamic interaction between it and a space-time environment

For example, he defined gravity **not** in terms of its rigidity but in terms of a dynamic interaction between a curvature in space and its energy density. For example, if one increases the energy density of a volume of space by adding mass it will increase its curvature.

One can understand why this would make the arrow of time irreversible by using an example of two dots on the surface of a balloon. The surface of the balloon will represent the "surface" of three-dimensional space and the "environment outside" of it will represent the time dimension in Einstein theories.

For example, if one applies energy by pushing down on its surface, it will change the spatial the configuration of the two dots. The change in its surface would be define not only by the distance it moves but by the direction it moves with respect to a fixed reference point.

One can us this to explain why time is irreversible in terms of a space-time environment if one assumes as many physicists do that it is a measure of sequential ordering of change caused by energy interacting with a space-time environment.

This is because if we removed the energy or pressure on the balloon the two dots would return to their original position. However, that removal causes the dots to move in the opposite direction from where it was applied and creating a new event with respect to the previous one.

But one would know that it did not travel back in time because the return to its original position is the next event in a sequence of events that defined its position.

The reason the laws of physics may **appear** to be reversible in an inertial reference frame when they are **not** is because they are not viewed from the perspective of the universe as a whole. This is because of the fact the rate observations tell us the universe expanding. Therefore, predictions made by reversing the laws physics will have a different energy content with respect to its origin.

Some may believe that arrow of time would be reversable if the expansion of universe was reversed. However, the random nature of its thermodynamic activity tells us it would not because due to that randomness each point would have a different energy content after is reversal than it had during its expansion.

Article 32
Should We Allow Mathematics to Be the Only Definition of Reality?

One thing all theoreticians especially physicists should be aware of is the fact there are many ways to mathematically quantify what we observe but only one can define the reality behind those observations.

History has shown assuming the existence of something based primarily on the quantitative powers of mathematics and not on observations of how an environment evolves can be misleading.

For example, many thought the Ptolemaic or geocentric system of planetary motion which used the mathematics of epicycles to explain the retrograde motion of the Moon, Sun, and planets was correct.

It was not until scientific investigations were stimulated by Copernicus's publication of his heliocentric theory and Galileo's observation of the phases of the moons of Jupiter did many European scientists consider the fact that it was not.

This is true even though many Greek, Indian and Muslim savants had published heliocentric hypotheses centuries before Copernicus.

However, why did it take almost two thousand years for them to realize their ideas were incorrect?

One reason may have been because the math that used epicycles was able to predict their positions within the observational tolerances of their equipment.

Yet, if the scientists who assumed the existence of epicycles had taken the time to observe the reality of how objects moved on earth, they would have realized there was a problem because, at least on earth, objects did **not** follow the curve path associated with epicycles.

However, because they were still able to make accurate mathematical predictions of a planet's position based on their existence, they were able to ignore those observations and suppress the more accurate Greek, Indian and Muslim ideas for almost 2000 years.

This suggests, the heliocentric or sun centered concept of planetary motion could have become the dominate paradigm long before 1610 if European scientists had not ignored the how of objects moved on earth.

Unfortunately, I do **not** believe many of today's physicists have learned that lesson.

For example, the proponents of Quantum Mechanics assume particles exist simultaneously exist in a superposition state as a particle and wave based solely on mathematical evolution the wave function.

However, observations of the environment we live in suggest that in reality particles **do not** exist in that state.

One can use those observation, the science of wave mechanics and the fact that Relativity tells us an electromagnetic wave moves continuously through space-time unless it is prevented from doing so by someone or something interacting with it. This would result in it being confined to three-dimensional space. The science of wave mechanics also tells us the three-dimensional "walls" of this confinement will result in its energy being reflected back on itself thereby creating a resonant or standing wave in three-dimensional space. This would cause its energy to be concentrated at a point in space were a particle would be found. Additionally, wave mechanics also tells us the energy of a resonant system such as a standing wave can only take on the discrete or quantized values associated with its fundamental or a harmonic of its fundamental frequency that the wave function associates with a particle.

Putting it in the thermology of Quantum Mechanics if an electromagnetic wave is

prevented from moving through space either by being observed or interacting with the external world its "Collapses" to a form a standing wave that would define the quantized energy Quantum Mechanics associates with a particle.

This suggests a particle does **may not simultaneously** exist as a particle and wave but is an entity with both the properties of a wave and a particle but not both at the same time.

The physicist Richard Feynman is credited with saying "The weird thing about Quantum Mechanics is that no one really understands it"

As was shown above one can understand why a quantum environment is what it is by observing how waves interact with the observable properties of our environment, we all live in instead of the unobservable one defines by the math of the wave function.

Scientists ESPECIALLY physicists should realize math is only a **tool** to quantify reality **not** a replacement for it.

Article 33
Should Allow Mathematics to Define Our Understanding of the Universe or Have it Define Our Mathematics?

Most of our modern sciences take their names from ancient Greek. In the case of physics, that word is "physik" which translates to "knowledge of nature and is dedicated to understanding how and why "our world behaves the way it does.

Proponents of this definition like Einstein focused on developing the mathematics to quantify **how** gravity interacts with its environment based on observations of how objects move along a curvature in the surface in our observable universe.

However, there is another definition of physics that assumes it should only have to quantify what we observe.

Proponents of this definition have developed a system of mathematics called Quantum Mechanics based on the mathematics of wave function which ONLY quantifies it but does not give a way to understand it in terms of observations. They assume the mathematical properties of the wave function only "**collapses**" or appears as a particle when it is observed or interacts with its environment.

However, we believe the ancient Greeks MAY not have felt comfortable using the term "physik" when referring to Quantum Mechanics a because as Bohr its founder said "If you are not completely confused by Quantum Mechanics, you do not (or cannot) understand it." in terms of observable properties of our universe.

Even so there are some proponents of Quantum Mechanics have suggested that because, to this date it is the only system that can accurately define the quantization of "our world" it MUST be product of that mathematical structure.

But the mathematics of Quantum Mechanics may not be the only way to define why we observe a quantum environment to behave the way it does.

For example, one can use mathematics to determine why we observe 4 apples on a table by assuming that originally there were two and two were added or there were six and two were taken away but only one of them defines how and why they actually are there.

This shows in most cases there are many ways to quantify both the number of apples on a table and what we observe in "our world".

This suggests we **may** be able to find another explanation other than the one provided for by Quantum Mechanics which can define why energy is quantize base on observations of its behavior in our universe.

For example, observations and Relativity tells us an electromagnetic wave moves continuously through space unless it is prevented from doing so by someone or something interacting with it. This would result in it being confined to three-dimensional space. The science of wave mechanics tells us the three-dimensional "walls" of this confinement will result in its energy being reflected back on itself thereby creating a resonant or standing wave in three-dimensional space. This would cause its energy to "**collapse**" or be concentrated at the point in space were a particle would be found. Additionally, wave mechanics also tells us the energy of a resonant system such as a standing wave can only take on the discrete or quantized values associated with its fundamental or a harmonic of its fundamental frequency that the wave function associates with a particle.

This not only explains one of the core principals of quantum theory that the wave function **only** presents itself as a particle when observed but also gives another avenue of research in finding a way to understand why the quantum environment behaves the way is does based on the observable properties of our universe.

As was mentioned earlier there are in most cases many ways to mathematically quantify what we observe in the universe. Therefore, we should not assume the solutions provided by Quantum Mechanics are the only ones that will make accurate predictions of its behavior.

What we as physicists and mathematicians **must** decide is should we allow math to define our understanding of existence or have it defined our math because it is possible a new system of math based on the behavior of "our world" could open doors to new technologies that will enable our civilization to advance beyond were one based on Quantum Mechanics can.

Article 34
Defining Quantum Gravity in terms of an emergent property of space-time.

Quantum Mechanics assumes the mathematical evolution of the wave function is responsible for the quantization of ALL mass and energy. Additionally, it assumes it exists in a superposition of several eigenstates and only reduces or "**collapses**" to a particle when it interacts with the external world. However, it has not been able to define how gravity is quantized in the same terms.

While Einstein defined gravity in terms of the how the energy density of space effects the geometry of space-time.

Therefore, one MAY be able to define a connection between Quantum Mechanics and Einstein's definition of gravity if one can define how and why it is concentrated in quantized unit of space-time in terms of its geometry.

But before we can begin, we need to establish a connection between the mathematical evolution of the wave function, its collapse and the derivation of gravity provided by Einstein.

This can be accomplished because in Relativity the evolution of space-time is the result of an electromagnetic wave while, as was mentioned earlier the wave function represent how a Quantum environment evolves to a particle.

This commonality suggests the wave function maybe represented by an electromagnetic wave in space-time. This means to derive the reason for its "collapse" in terms of space-time one must physically connect its evolution to it.

This can be done by using the science of wave mechanics and Relativity because they tell us an electromagnetic wave moves continuously through space-time unless it is prevented from doing so by its interaction with an observer or its environment. The science of wave mechanics also tells us the three-dimensional "walls" of this confinement will result in its energy being reflected back on itself thereby creating a resonant or standing wave in three-dimensional space. Additionally, wave mechanics also tells us the energy of a resonant system such as a standing wave can only take on the discrete or quantized values associated with its fundamental or a harmonic of its fundamental frequency that the wave function associates with a particle.

This shows how Relativity can provide a Classical explanation for one of the core principals of

Quantum Mechanics in that when field properties light or wave properties of all other forms of energy in a space-time environment are prevented from moving through it either by being observed or encountering an object that energy will be observed in the quantized in the form of a particle.

As was mentioned earlier Einstein defined gravity in terms of how the energy density of space effects the geometry of space-time. Therefore, assuming as was done above that a particle is composed of a resonate standing wave in three-dimensional space means the increase or decreases of the energy density of space can only be in quantized units associated with its resonant frequency of the particles a mass contains. Therefore, because Einstein defined gravity in terms of the energy density of space means he also defined why it is quantized.

This suggests the quantization of gravity is an emergent property of space-time because one can use the science wave mechanics and observations to define why the energy density of a space-time environment can only take on the discrete or quantized values associated with its fundamental or a harmonic of its fundamental frequency.

Article 35
Why Finding a Theory of Everything is so Difficult.

The definition of a Theory of Everything is that it should completely define the physical properties of our universe. However, before we begin, we should first determine how we what to do that. In other words, do we want find a universal equation to quantify what we observe or explain why we observe it or **both.**

For example, Quantum Mechanics **only** quantifies observations of the environment it defines in terms of the mathematically properties of a wave function. It was developed by using the numerical value of observations to define a wavefunction that predicts those values.

Einstein took a different approach when developing Relativity. He first sought to understand and explain how and why the speed of light is constant despite the relative motion of an observer in terms of how things in our observable universe would interact if that were true. He then developed the math to quantify his explanation.

Both of these theories can be part of a theory of everything however that is only possible if they both define the universe we occupy.

For example, one can use mathematics to determine why we observe 4 apples on a table in a dark room before the light are turned on by assuming that originally there were 2 on it and 2 were added or there were 6 and 2 were taken away.

However, there is no way using math alone to determine how many apples existed before they were observed on the table.

But if we know the weight of the apples on the table, we could determine the average weight of an apple by weighing and counting the number in a bushel. We could use that information to determine how many of them were present before the lights were turned on.

As was mentioned earlier Quantum Mechanics **only** quantifies observations of environment it defines in terms of the mathematically properties of a wave function. This means it may define a universe that we do not live even though it can accurately quantify it.

This is because, as with the apples a mathematical solution cannot confirm its assumption that the wavefunction defines our universe.

However, if one does as Einstein did and first try to explain how and why we observed what we do in terms of how things interact in our observable environment and then based those observations, one derives the mathematics to predict and quantify those observation we are more apt to define the universe we are a part of.

This suggests if one takes approach the Einstein did in developing Relativity and applied it to the fact that energy is quantized one may be able to derive a Theory of Everything that not only quantifies observations of our environment but also explain how and why they do in terms of them.

For example, in "our universe" observations, the science of wave mechanics and Relativity tells us waves such as an electromagnetic one moves continuously through space-time unless it is prevented from doing so by someone or something interacting with it. This would result in it being confined to a volume of three-dimensional space. The science of wave mechanics also tells us the three-dimensional "walls" of this confinement will result in its energy being reflected back on itself thereby creating a resonant or standing wave in three-dimensional space. This would cause its energy to be concentrated at the point in space were a particle would be found. Additionally, wave mechanics also tells us the energy of a resonant system such as a standing wave can only take on the discrete or quantized values associated with its fundamental or a harmonic of its fundamental frequency that the wave function associates with a particle.

This means one does not have to assume that the mathematics of the wavefunction is the only reason why mass and energy is quantized. This is because as was shown above one can **not only** quantify it but explain why using the observable properties of our environment.

However, this suggests we may be able to find a Theory of Everything if we **not only** attempt to mathematically quantize what we observe but attempt to understand and explain why we observe it based on how the components of our observable environment interact.

Article 36
Reality Is What It Is
Not What Mathematics
tell us It Can Be.

Objective reality is defined as something that is established by consensus and is consider actual and independent of the mind.

However, all proponents of quantum theory believe that it does not exist because they assume only the abstract one defined by the mathematics of the wavefunction does.

Yet Schrodinger developed the wavefunction based on the quantitative observations of our environment based on the **objective reality** of those observations. However, if they did not exist, he would not have been able to define the wavefunction.

The question we need to answer is should we assume that **objective reality does not exist** based solely on a mathematical definition such as Quantum Mechanics does if that math is based on its existence.

One of the primary reasons why so many do so is because they assume it is the only to define why our objective reality is what it is.

However, there is a problem basing the existence of an environment as quantum mechanics does purely on mathematics.

Briefly if you were asked to predict why we observed two apples on a table in a dark room you could say that there are 4 apples and 2 were taken away or there were 6 and four were removed. However, both give a correct prediction of what we observe however only one correctly defines its reality. One way to determine which one does would be to observe their environment.

Granted we may not be able to do so in the dark but if we could weight them, we could determine how many there were by dividing the weight of a bushel of them by the number in it to determine the average weight of one. This would provide way to determine how many there were on the table by dividing their total weigh by the average weigh of one.

This would connect the subjective reality of the math used to define the number of apples on the table to the objective one defined by the number in a bushel.

There little doubt that Quantum Mechanics makes extremely accurate predictions of the observable properties of its environment however the reality it defines is incompatible with the classical one we can observe.

One way to distinguish which one is correct would be to observe how the components of our objective reality interact and determine if they can explain why a quantum environment behaves the way it does.

For example, one can use the science of wave mechanics and the fact we can observe electromagnetic waves move continuously through space unless it is prevented from doing so by being observer or interacting with an object to explain why matter and energy is quantized.

This is because the science of wave mechanics also tells us the three-dimensional "walls" of this confinement will result in its energy being reflected back on itself thereby creating a resonant or standing wave in three-dimensional space. Additionally, wave mechanics also tells us the energy of a resonant system such as a standing wave can only take on the discrete or quantized values associated with its fundamental or a harmonic of its fundamental frequency that the wave function associates with a particle.

This is essentially how Quantum Mechanics defines the reality of its environment because it tells us that a particle only appears when interacts with an observer or its environment.

Yet as was show above one can explain how and why it does so in terms of the objective properties of classical environment by observing how the components of classical environment interact to create it.

This is why, as was mentioned earlier we should never accept a definition of the reality our universe based **only** on the abstract properties of mathematics if one can as was shown above based it on the objective properties of an environment because reality is what it is not what mathematics tells is it can be.

Article 37
Why Our Universe is Asymmetrical With Respect to Time and the Laws of Physics.

Einstein gave us the following reasons why our universe is asymmetric with respect to time and the laws of physics when he defined change in terms of an interaction between space and energy.

But before we can understand **why** we must first define what time is.

Many define it in the abstract saying it is an invention of the human mind that gives us a sense of order, a before and after so to speak. However, many physicists also define it in terms of the physical properties of a space-time dimension.

However, Einstein provided an explanation for the changes associated with the passage of time when he defined it in terms of a dynamic interaction between space and energy because it gives us a physical mechanism for defining why it occurs.

One can use an example of two dots on the surface of a balloon to understand why.

The "surface" of the balloon will represent the "surface" of three-dimensional space and the three-dimensions outside of it will represent the time dimension in Einstein theories.

If one uses energy to push down on its surface, it will change the spatial configuration of the two dots. The change in its surface would be defined not only by the distance it moves but by the direction.

However, if the internal air pressure increases or decreases its entire surface as measured from its center will also move with respect to the three-dimensional space surrounding it.

Since there are two components to measuring change in a spatial environment, one in terms of its direction and the other in terms of its sequential ordering one should assume the same would be true in a space-time environment.

As was mentioned earlier, Einstein defined the change associate with time in terms of a dynamic interaction between energy and space. For example, the energy of a rocket will change the configuration of the "surface" of three-dimensional space with respect to the time dimension. This means, similar to the balloon he defined change in terms of its dynamic properties.

However, Einstein also define two different environments for change associated with time when he defined the properties of inertial reference frames. One is the reference frame itself and the other is reference organ of the universe

For example, he defined an inertial reference frames as encapsulated regions of space which do not experience any external forces.

This means they laws of physics **are** symmetrical with respect to time in terms inertial reference fames because starting and end point of their predictions are referenced to it and not referenced to the center of the universe its expansion or contraction. Therefore, they will be **always** be symmetrical with respect to them.

However, the starting and end points of their reversal will be different of all interrail reference frame with respect to the origins of the universe due to its expansion. Therefore, will always have different energy content and will be asymmetric.

Article 38
Particle spins in terms of four-dimensional space-time.

When certain elementary particles move through a magnetic field, they are deflected or "spin" in a manner that suggests they have the properties of little magnets.

To explain how a property of four-dimensional space-time is responsible one must first understand how its spatial properties interact to create an electromagnetic field.

Einstein in his General Theory of Relativity defined the forces associated with gravity in terms of a geometric curvature in space-time whose force vector perpendicular to the other two-dimensional plains it intersects.

However, that does **not** mean the other two axis of three-dimensional space cannot contribute to energy content of space.

In his formulation of electromagnetism Maxwell described light as a propagating electromagnetic wave created by the interaction of its electric and magnetic fields.

It can and will be shown the electric and magnetic component of an electromagnetic wave are the result of a spatial displacement in either one of the two dimensional plains that are perpendicular to gravity force vector.

One can understand the mechanism responsible by using the analogy of how a wave on the two-dimensional surface of water causes a point on that surface to become displaced or rise above or below the equilibrium point that existed before the wave was present.

The science of wave mechanics tells us a force would be developed by these displacements which will result in the elevated and depressed portions of the water moving towards or becoming "attracted" to each other and the surface of the water.

Similarly, an electromagnetic wave on one of the "surfaces" of the two spatial dimensions that are perpendicular to the axis of gravitational force vector would cause a point on that "surface" to become displaced or rise above and below the equilibrium point that existed before the wave was present.

Therefore, classical wave mechanics, if extrapolated to the properties of two of the three spatial dimensions tells us a force will be developed by the differential displacements caused by an electromagnetic wave on it which will result in the elevated and depressed portions moving towards or become "attracted" to each other as the wave moves through space.

This defines the causality of the attractive electrical fields that Maxwell associated with an electromagnetic wave in terms of a force caused by the alternating displacements of a wave on a "surface" either one of the two dimensional plains that are perpendicular to gravities force vector.

However, it also provides a classical mechanism for understanding why similar electrical fields of an electromagnetic wave repel each other. This is because observations of waves show there is a direct relationship between the magnitude of a displacement in its "surface" to the magnitude of the force resisting that displacement.

Similarly, the magnitude of a displacement in a "surface" of either one of the two dimensional plains that are perpendicular gravities force vector by two similar electrical fields will be greater than that caused by a single one. Therefore, they will repel each other the force resisting the displacement will be greater for them than it would be for a single one.

One can also derive the magnetic component of an electromagnetic field in terms of the horizontal force developed along the axis that is perpendicular to the displacement caused by its peaks and troughs associated with the electric fields. This would be analogous to how the perpendicular displacement of a mountain generates a horizontal force on the surface of the earth, which pulls matter horizontally towards the apex of that displacement.

This explain why the electrical and magnetic fields of an electromagnetic wave are in phase or maximum at the same time.

As was shown above the science of wave mechanics allows one to explain the how the electric and magnetic forces interact to form an electromagnetic wave by assuming it is moving through time on the "surface" of the two-dimensional plains of space-time that is perpendicular to the line of action of gravitational forces.

However, to understand how the spin properties of a particle are a related to the geometry of four-dimensional space-time one must first explain the origin of the quantized properties of particles in terms of an electromagnetic wave.

One way of doing this is to use the fact that evolution in a space-time environment is, in part defined by electromagnetic waves.

For example, the science of wave mechanics along with the fact that Relativity tells us wave energy moves continuously through space-time unless it is prevented from doing so by someone or something interacting with it. This would result in its energy being confined to three-dimensional space. The science of wave mechanics also tells us the three-dimensional "walls" of this confinement will result in its energy being reflected back on itself thereby creating a resonant or standing wave in three-dimensional space. This would cause its wave energy to be concentrated at the point in space were a particle would be found. Additionally, wave mechanics also tells us the energy of a resonant system, such as a standing wave can only take on the discrete or quantized values associated with its fundamental or a harmonic of its fundamental frequency. This defines how and why the field properties of an electromagnetic wave evolves to become a photon in a space-time environment.

The fact all particles are observed to have a wave component strongly suggests the above mechanism is responsible for their quantization as well as a photon.

This also provides a Classical explanation for one of the core principals of Quantum Mechanics in that when the field properties light or wave properties of all forms of energy are prevented from moving through space either by being observed or encountering an object that energy will be observed in the quantized in the form of a particle.

However, if the quantum properties of all particles are the result of standing wave as is suggested above its magnetic component when interacting with an electromagnetic field will have two possible orientations which are perpendicular to each other. This is because, as was shown above the magnetic field of an electromagnetic energy can be directed along either one of the two-dimensional plains that are perpendicular to gravity force vector.

However, this means there would be only two possible ways in which a particle can spin after interacting an electromagnetic field because there

are only two ways it can orient itself with respect to the three spatial dimensions of space-time.

Article 39
Why an electron does not fall into the nucleus in terms of the strong and weak nuclear forces

It can be shown one may able to derive the strong and weak nuclear forces and the internal geometry of protons and neutrons in terms of the orientation of axes of the dimensional components of space similar to the way Einstein defined the force of gravity in terms of how a curvature in space reoriented them.

Observations of hadrons such as protons and neutrons confirmed they are made up of distinct components called quarks of which there are six types, the UP/Down, Charm/Strange and Top/Bottom. The Up, Charm and Top have a fractional charge of 2/3 while the Down, Strange and Bottom have a fractional charge of -1/3.

However, another property of quarks defined by Quantum Chromodynamics (QCD), is their color charge which are red, green, and blue. It assumes each one is made up of three different colors of quarks red, blue and green and only the combinations of the colors that produce "white" can be found in a stable particle.

Observations have shown that each proton is made of three quarks, with two up quarks and one down quark. Neutrons have two down quarks and one up quark.

Yet, no one has been able to define how they combine to form their internal structure in terms of Einstein's theories.

However, it can and will be shown their internal structure can be defined if one assumes the color charge of each quark represents orientation of the two-dimensional plains of three-dimensional space (xy, yz, xz).

For example, red would represent the xy plane, green, the yz, and blue xz. The fact that three-dimensional space contains **only** one of each explains why a particle must be composed of one each color to be stable in our spatial environment.

It can also explain why their fractional charges are in thirds because, as was shown in detail in the Article 45 "Defining Maxwells Equation in terms of the physical properties of space-time" (page 217) their electrical potential is related to a displacement of one of the three-dimensional plains with respect to the other two of three-dimensional space.

This suggests the 2/3 fractional charge of the Up, Charm and Top quarks MAY be the result of the orientation of their two-dimensional planes with respect to the 1/3 fractional charge of the Down, Strange and Bottom quarks.

This would allow one understand the internal structure of protons and neutrons in terms of the fact that our universe is made up of **only** three spatial dimensions. Therefore, for a proton or neutron to be stable in it can only contain properties of the xy, yz, and xz dimensional plains.

If they are not, they will be unstable.

For example, the two up quarks of a proton each with a positive fractional charge of two would contain 4 two-dimensional plains (one for each charge). However, Einstein showed us each dimensional plane can reorient itself with respect to the others.

This tells us the dimensional plain associated with the negative fractional charge of one of its up quarks can be reoriented to oppose one of the positive ones carried by one of the dimensional plains of the up quarks. This means a proton will have 3 of 4 dimensional plains associated with the 2 up quarks.

This will form a stable structure in three-dimensional space because it contains only the (xy, yz, xz) plains Additionally, it will result in it having the positive charge of a proton because it will present only 1 of the +2/3 positive charges of their two up quarks.

The strong nuclear force is related to the fact the energy required to reorient the dimensional planes of one of the down quarks of a proton is less than that required to have them individually exist in our three-dimensional universe. Therefore, the magnitude of the strong nuclear force would be equal to the difference between those two states.

Neutrons on the other hand contain one up quark and two down quarks. It is neutral because the 2 -1/3 fractional charge of each of the two down quarks orient themselves to oppose +2/3 charges of the up quarks.

This suggests the reason a proton is stable and a neutron is not is because it takes more energy to reorient the two two-dimensional plains of a neutron than one of the dimensional plains of a proton.

However, this also suggest the reason a neutron is stable **only** in the nucleus is because it must "borrow" enough binding energy from a proton to reorient the two-dimensional plains associated with the two down quarks to oppose those of the up quark. This would make it neutral with respect to their charge.

Yet a neutron is unstable and decays into an electron and neutrino when it is outside of the nucleus because it does not have enough internal energy to keep the dimensional components of its quarks in three-dimensional space.

The weak nuclear force acts inside of individual nucleons, which has a shorter range than the strong force. It is the force that allows protons to turn into neutrons and vice versa through beta decay.

The reason for this is when it is it is inside of the nucleus it can borrow some of the excess binding energy of proton to enable it to be stable.

However, when it is outside of the nucleus three of the four dimensional plains associated with its quark's components return to their original configuration creating empty space. The remaining dimensional plain associated with either one of the two down quarks would orient itself so that it would cancel the positive charge of the proton resulting in the creation of an electron and thereby maintain the charge balance of the universe. The energy of the neutrino would represent what it had to borrow from the proton to maintain it stability.

This suggests the reason an electron does not fall into the nucleus is because it would take more energy to do so than it would take to remain outside of it.

Additionally, the reason a proton can become a neutron when a neutrino collides with it in an atom is because it transfers enough energy to the proton to reorient the one of the two-dimensional plains associated with its two down quarks to oppose those of the up quark.

Article 40
A background independent quantum gravity in terms of Relativity.

Background independence is a condition in theoretical physics that requires the defining equations of a theory to be independent of the actual shape of its environment and the value of various fields within it.

In particular this means that it must be possible to define the laws of physic in a manner that does not refer to a specific coordinate system. In addition, the different configurations (or backgrounds) should be obtained as different solutions of the underlying equations.

Einstein accomplished this when he defined gravity and the shape or geometry of space-time in terms of its energy density while defining the interaction of gravitating bodies in terms of a gravity wave moving through space. Therefore, to define a background independent quantum gravity one must first show why its energy is quantized and then show why it is independent of the geometry and the value of the various fields within the spacetime environment it occupies.

Relativity and the science of wave mechanics tells us wave energy moves continuously through space-time unless it is prevented from doing so by someone or something interacting with it. This would result in its energy being confined to three-dimensional space. The science of wave mechanics also tells us the three-dimensional "walls" of this confinement will result in its energy being reflected back on itself thereby creating a resonant or standing wave in three-dimensional space. This would cause its wave energy to be concentrated at the point in space were a particle would be found. Additionally, wave mechanics also tells us the energy of a resonant system, such as a standing wave can only take on the discrete or quantized values associated with its fundamental or a harmonic of its fundamental frequency.

This defines how and why the field properties of space-time **can** evolve to create a quantized increase in the energy density and therefore gravity in a space-time environment.

This suggests the quantization of gravity is not a fundamental property of space but an emergent property of property of space-time.

As was mentioned earlier Einstein defined gravity and the shape or geometry of space-time in terms of its energy density. However as was shown above it would be background independent because the location of a quantized unit of energy does not to refer to a specific coordinate system and therefore coordinate-free with respect to the space-time geometry.

However, some feel that gravity is not because the fact that gravity waves cause acceleration when they interact with objects which they feel suggests they are background dependent because they change geometry of space as they move through it.

Yet this is not true because gravity waves are the result of the two accelerating gravitating masses interacting with each other. This suggests they should obey the same laws that govern the energy waves of all accelerated reference frames which Einstein showed in GR are not background independent.

Therefore, the fact that gravity waves cause acceleration when they interact with objects is expected because they are a result of an interaction of two accelerated reference frames.

However as was mentioned earlier the gravitational forces associated with a non-accelerated mass would be background independent with respect to the geometry of space-time because as was shown earlier the equations defining the resonant standing wave which defined the quantum properties energy is independent of the shape of spacetime and the value of various fields within it.

Article 41
Defining Quantum gravity in terms of an emergent property of space-time.

For close to a century physicist have been attempting to define how gravity is quantized in terms of it being a fundamental property of our universe without success. However, as will be shown below its quantum properties can be define in terms of an emergent property of space-time.

One can use the science of wave mechanics, the fact that Einstein defined gravity in terms of the energy density of space-time and the observations that waves energy move continuously through it unless it is prevented from doing so by someone or something interacting with it. This would result in its energy being confined to three-dimensional space. The science of wave mechanics also tells us the three-dimensional "walls" of this confinement will result in its energy being reflected back on itself thereby creating a resonant or standing wave in three-dimensional space. This would cause its wave energy to be concentrated at the point in space were a particle would be found. Additionally, wave mechanics also tells us the energy of a resonant system, such as a standing wave can only take on the discrete or quantized values associated with a fundamental or a harmonic of its fundamental frequency.

This defines how and why the field properties of a space-time environment can evolve to create a quantized increase in its energy density.

As was mentioned earlier Einstein defined gravity and the shape or geometry of space-time in terms of its energy density and because its energy density is quantized gravity it is too.

This suggests the quantization of gravity **may** not be a fundamental but an emergent property of our universe caused by an interaction between energy and the continuous field properties of space-time.

Article 42
What supports the geometry of "empty" space-time?

When Einstein defined the equivalence between mass and energy, he also defined what "supports" the geometry of space-time.

In his General Theory of Relativity, he defined the force of gravity in terms of the energy density of space. This implies energy supports the geometric structure space because it tells us when energy is concentrated in the form of mass it causes the geometry of space to contract creating the curvature he associated with gravity.

Additionally, the Big Bang's assumption the universe expansion is the result of the energy associated with its origin can only be explained by assuming it is pushing on its boundaries.

This is supported by fact we can observed that the CBM (Cosmic Background Radiation) imparts the energy associated with its 2.725 Kelvin temperature to even perfectly "empty" space devoid of all gas, dust, and particular matter.

The mechanism responsible would be analogous to how the volume of a balloon is supported by the air inside of it.

For example, it is the thermodynamic energy of the air molecules that support its volume not the mass of the particles of air in inside of it.

This suggests the energy imparted the 2.725 Kelvin temperature of the CBM to evenly perfectly "empty" space devoid of all gas, dust, and particular matter; is what supports the geometry of space-time.

Article 43
A Classical explanation of the delayed choice quantum eraser experiment in terms of space-time

There is a classical explanation for the results of the delayed choice quantum eraser experiment in terms of interaction of the individual photons with the properties of the experimental setup.

It is discovered, using the setup described in in Figure 6 an interference pattern is generated by a photon striking detector 1 and 3. However, the photons striking the detectors 2 and 4 do not produce one. This is true even though all of the photon used in the experiment are identical.

Many believe the result of this experiment verify Quantum Mechanics assumption of the duality or wave and particle properties of a photon because as was mentioned in a Wikipedia article "If a photon manifests itself as though it had come by a single path to the detector, then "common sense" says that it must have entered the double-slit device as a *particle*. If a photon manifests itself as though it had come by two indistinguishable paths, then it must have entered the double-slit device as a *wave*".

However as was shown in the earlier discussion of the double silt experiment "Article 21 The Double Slit Experiment in Space-time." (**Page 105**) the appearance of an interference pattern on the screen can be classically explained in term of a standing wave that would be created when an electromagnetic wave is preventing from moving freely through space-time.

Briefly the double slit experiment is made up of a coherent source of photons illuminating a screen after passing through a thin plate with two parallel slits cut in it. Their wave properties cause them to create an interference pattern of bright and dark bands on the screen. However, at the screen, the light is always found to be absorbed as discrete particles, called photons.

However, the fact that it was always absorbed as a particle made it necessary to go beyond classical physics and take the quantum nature of light into account.

The most puzzling part of this experiment occurs when only one photon at a time impacts a barrier with two opened slits because an interference pattern forms which is similar to what it was when multiple photons were impacting the barrier. This is a clear implication the particle called a photon has a wave component, which simultaneously passes through both slits and interferes with itself. (The experiment works with electrons, atoms, and even some molecules too.)"

Many believe the importance of this experiment is that it demonstrates both the duality of the wave and particle properties of photons and the concepts of superposition and quantum interference.

Yet, one can understand this experiment in terms of the classical properties of our environment defined by the science of wave mechanics and Relativity. This is because they tell us an electromagnetic wave moves continuously through space unless it is prevented from doing so by someone observing or something interacting with it. This would result in its energy being confined in three-dimensional space. The science of wave mechanics also tells us the three-dimensional "walls" of this confinement will result in its energy being reflected back on itself thereby creating a resonant standing wave in three-dimensional space. This would cause its energy to be concentrated at the point in space where a particle would be found. Additionally, wave mechanics also tells us the energy of a resonant system, such as a standing wave which this confinement would create can only take on the discrete or quantized values associated with its fundamental or a harmonic of its fundamental frequency.

Additionally, it also tells us a particle would have an extended volume equal to the wavelength associated with its standing wave.

Putting it in the vernacular of Quantum Mechanics when an electromagnetic wave is prevented from moving through space either by being observed or encountering an object it "Collapses" to a form a standing wave that would define the quantized energy Quantum Mechanics associates with a particle.

It shows why the interference pattern remains when one photon at a time is fired at the barrier with both slits open or the most puzzling part of this experiment is because, as mentioned earlier it is made up of an electromagnetic wave, therefore it occupies an extended volume which is directly related to the wavelength of its standing wave.

This means a portion of its energy could simultaneously pass both slits, if the diameter of its volume exceeds the separation of the slits and recombine on the other side to generate an interference pattern.

However, when its energy is prevented from moving through space by contacting the screen it will be will confined to three-dimensional space causing it to be concentrated in a standing wave that as mentioned earlier would define energy of the photon that impacted the screen.

As was mentioned earlier it was discovered using the delayed choice quantum eraser setup described in in figure 6 an interference pattern is generated by photon striking detector 1 and 3. However the photons striking detectors 2 of the 4 screens do not produce one. This is true even all of the photon used in the experiment are identical.

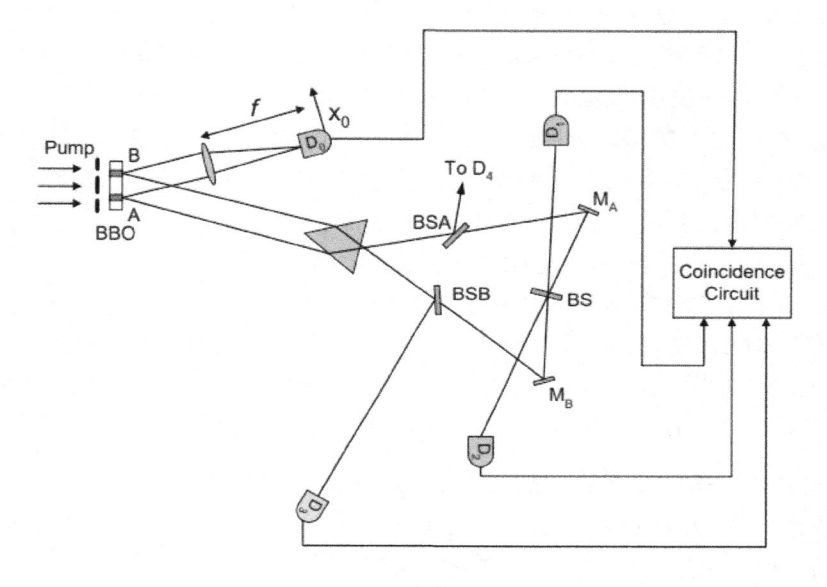

Figure 6

Diagram of the delayed choice quantum eraser experiment

The experimental setup, described in detail in Kim is illustrated in Fig 4. An argon laser generates individual 351.1 nm photons that pass through a double-slit apparatus (vertical black line in the upper left corner of the diagram).

An individual photon goes through one (or both) of the two slits. In the illustration, the photon paths are color-coded as red or light blue lines to indicate which slit the photon came through (red indicates slit A, light blue indicates slit B).

So far, the experiment is like a conventional two-slit experiment. However, after the slits, spontaneous parametric down-conversion (SPDC) is used to prepare an entangled two-photon state. This is done by a nonlinear optical crystal BBO (beta barium borate) that converts the photon (from either slit) into two identical, orthogonally polarized entangled photons with 1/2 the frequency of the original photon. The paths followed by these orthogonally polarized photons are caused to diverge by the Glan–Thompson prism.

One of these 702.2 nm photons, referred to as the "signal" photon (look at the red and light-blue lines going upwards from the Glan–Thompson prism) continues to the target detector called D_0. During an experiment, detector D_0 is scanned along its x axis, its motions controlled by a step motor. A plot of "signal" photon counts detected by D_0 versus x can be examined to discover whether the cumulative signal forms an interference pattern.

The other entangled photon, referred to as the "idler" photon (look at the red and light-blue lines going downwards from the Glan–Thompson prism), is deflected by prism PS that sends it along divergent paths depending on whether it came from slit A or slit B.

Somewhat beyond the path split, the idler photons encounter beam splitters BS_a, BS_b, and BS_c that each have a 50% chance of allowing the idler photon to pass through and a 50% chance of causing it to be reflected. M_a and M_b are mirrors

However as was shown in the earlier discussion of the double silt experiment the appearance of a photon on the screen **can be define** in terms of a classical property of an electromagnetic wave which causes it to create standing wave if preventing from moving freely through space-time.

Additionally, because the energy of the standing wave which earlier was shown to define the quantum properties of a photon is dependent on its frequency each individual photon will occupy a unique place on the screen where the interference creates the energy associated with a standing wave of that frequency.

However, one can define a classical explanation for the shape of diffraction patterns shown in Figure 7 because it tells us the random thermodynamic energy of the mirrors used to change the paths of the D1 and D2 photons will result in randomization as was mentioned earlier of their frequency resulting in them forming the wave patterns on the left side of the Figure 7

However, the photons 3 and 4 which do not contact any mirrors will not be randomized and

therefore will produce the pattern on the right side of that figure.

This tells us classical wave mechanics can explain why the shape of inference pattern created on the screen is the result of the peaks and valleys of the interference pattern of each individual photon overlapping as shown in figure 7

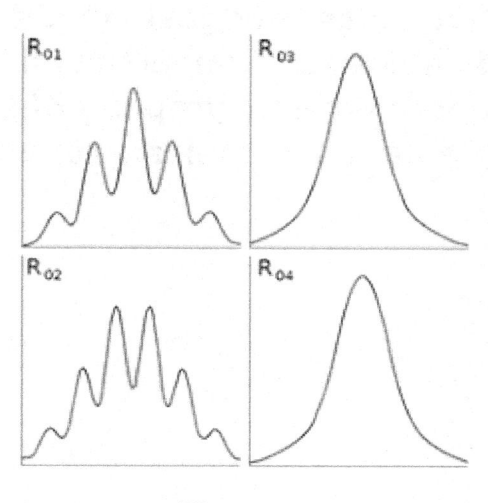

Figure 7

This suggest the reason the results of the delayed choice quantum eraser experiment are what they are is due the classical properties of space-time and the physical properties of the experimental setup and **not** the quantum mechanical properties of a photon.

Some may say because of the deterministic properties of a classical environment each photon that interacts with the components of the experimental setup will have the same energy. However classical physics also tells the random thermodynamic energy in each of those components will result in random fluctuations in the energy of the photons that interact with them.

But the fact the photons that took the path D1 and D4 that interacted with the mirror have the same interference pattern while the ones that did not did not share that pattern suggests that the results of the delayed choice experiment may be due to a classical thermodynamic property of the mirrors and not a quantum mechanical property of photons

Article 44
Merging the properties of Quantum Mechanics and Relativity to resolve the measurement problem.

In Quantum Mechanics, the **measurement problem** is how to connect the mathematical and probabilistic interpretation of the wave function to the classical properties of position and momentum. The fact that we cannot observe it has given rise to different interpretations and poses a key set of questions that each interpretation must answer.

One solution is called Quantum Decoherence or the process in which a system's behavior changes from one which can be explained by mathematics of the wave function to one that can be explained by classical mechanics when it is measured or interacts with its external environment.

However, it even though it does provide a framework for the classical environment of particles in terms of the quantum properties of a system it does not define how or why that occurs.

Yet one can explain why if one assumes the wavefunction symbolizes the interaction of the classically observable properties of an electromagnetic wave with those of Einstein's space-time environment.

For example, the science of wave mechanics along with the fact that Relativity tells us an electromagnetic wave moves continuously through space-time unless it is prevented from doing so by being observed or interacting with its environment. This would result in its energy being confined to three-dimensional space. The science of wave mechanics also tells us the three-dimensional "walls" of this confinement will result in its energy being reflected back on itself thereby creating a resonant or standing wave in three-dimensional space. This would cause its wave energy to be concentrated at the point in space were a particle would be found. Additionally, wave mechanics also tells us the energy of a resonant system, such as a standing wave can only take on the discrete or quantized values associated with its fundamental or a harmonic of its fundamental frequency.

Yet this is similar to how the wavefunction defines the evolution of its environment in the sense that its wave properties **only** become a quantized particle in a classical environment when observed or interacting with its environment.

However, it also explains why a particle has volume instead of a mathematical point as defined by mathematics of the wavefunction is because it is made up of the classical properties of a standing wave which would define its spatial extent.

As was mentioned earlier the wavefunction also defines the position of a particle in terms of probabilities which many believe is inconsistent which the classical properties of determinism.

However, classical physical physics also defines the position of object or particle in terms of mathematical point which defines the center of mass.

This allows one to define the **apparent** determinism of classical environment in terms of the probabilities of a quantum one.

For example, the probabilistic interpretation of the wave function is **necessary** (in part) because Quantum Mechanics cannot define the exact point representing center of the standing wave which earlier defined a particle.

Therefore, the randomness of where that point is with respect to a particle's center will result in its position, when observed to be randomly distributed in its environment. This means one must define where it appears in terms of probabilities to average the deviations that are caused by the random placement of that point.

Similarly, the science of thermodynamics tells us the point called the center gravity will be randomly displaced by the thermal energy of the object it is a part of. Therefore, to determine the exact position of the center of gravity in a classical environment one must use thermodynamics probabilities which define when a specific change will occur in a classical environment.

However, it also means that a classical environment is similar to quantum one in that it must use probabilities to define the exact position of particle or object.

This suggests that Quantum Mechanics and Relativity are computable even though they operate in different environments. Quantum Mechanics use a probabilistic mathematical environment to define the point where a particle is found while Relativity uses, as was mentioned earlier a thermodynamic probability to define the exact position of the point called the center of gravity of and object in a space-time universe.

Therefore, because one can, as was shown above explain the probabilities of a quantum environment in terms of a relativistic one and the classical properties of relativistic environment in terms of a quantum one, maybe should look for ways in which we can merge them in to a theory which can define all aspects of our universe instead of attempting to do so using **only** one of the other.

Article 45
Defining Maxwells Equation in terms of the physical properties of space-time.

In Maxwell's mathematical formulation of electromagnetism, he defined light as a propagating electromagnetic wave created by the interaction of its electric and magnetic fields

While Einstein in his General Theory of Relativity defined the forces associated with gravity in terms of a geometric curvature or spatial displacement in space-time caused by its energy density.

Additionally, he showed it was directed along the radius of the curvature in the two-dimensional plane that was parallel to it.

Therefore, to explain how Maxwells equations can be defined in terms of a space-time environment one must show how both the observable and mathematical properties of an electromagnetic waves: such as why they made up of electric and magnetic fields and why polarized light has a perpendicular orientation in terms of the geometry of space-time. Additionally, one must also show why its electrical and magnetic components are in phase, it's the only thing that can move at the speed of light along with the defining the reason why it always appears as a photon when observed or interacts with its environment in terms of that same geometry.

As was just mentioned Gravity's force vector was defined by Einstein as being along the radius of one of dimensional plains of three-dimensional space. However, that does **not** mean the other two plains of three-dimensional space cannot support the energy associated with electromagnetic energy.

The fact that light is polarized supports that assumption because it allows one to understand its perpendicular orientation in terms energy waves moving on one of either of the two-dimensional plains that are perpendicular to each other.

However, as will be shown below it will also allow one to explain both the propagation of light and Maxwell equations if one assumes its electrical and magnetic components are the result of the displacements created by its peaks and troughs of an electromagnetic wave on one those two-dimensional plains.

The conjecture a displacement created by a wave on either one of the two-dimensional planes of three-dimension space can be responsible for the propagation of electromagnetic energy is consistent with General Relativity's assumption a spatial displacement in them is responsible gravitational energy.

One can understand the mechanism responsible by using the analogy of how a wave on the two-dimensional surface of water causes a point on that surface to become displaced or rise above or below the equilibrium point that existed before the wave was present.

The science of wave mechanics tells us a force would be developed by those displacements which would result in the elevated and depressed portions of the water moving towards or becoming "attracted" to each other and the surface of the water.

Similarly, an electromagnetic wave on the "surface" on one of the two spatial dimensions that are perpendicular to the axis of gravitational forces would cause a point on that "surface" to become displaced or rise above and below the equilibrium point that existed before the wave was present.

Therefore, classical wave mechanics, if extrapolated to two of the three spatial dimensions of our universe that are perpendicular to the one responsible for gravity tells us a force will be developed by the differential displacements of electromagnetic wave which will result in its elevated and depressed portions moving towards or become "attracted" to each other as the wave moves through space.

This would define the causality of the attractive electrical fields associated with an electromagnetic wave in terms of a force caused by the alternating displacements of a wave moving with respect to time on a "surface" of the two spatial dimensions which are perpendicular to the axis of gravitational forces.

However, it also provides a classical mechanism for understanding why similar electrical fields repel each other. This is because observations of waves show there is a direct relationship between the magnitude of a displacement in its "surface" to the magnitude of the force resisting that displacement.

Similarly, the magnitude of multiple displacements in a "surface" of a two-dimensional plain in space-time will be greater than that caused by a single one. Therefore, they will repel each other because the magnitude of the force resisting the displacement will be greater than it would be for a single one.

One can also derive the magnetic component of an electromagnetic wave in terms of the horizontal force developed along the axis that is perpendicular to the displacement caused by its peaks and troughs associated with the electric fields.

This would be analogous to how the perpendicular displacement of a mountain generates a horizontal force on the surface of the earth, which pulls matter horizontally towards the apex of that displacement.

This also explain why the electrical and magnetic fields of an electromagnetic wave are in phase or maximum at the same time in terms of the geometric properties of space-time defined by Einstein.

However, it also provides an explanation for why electromagnetic waves can transmit energy through space at the speed of light.

The observations and the science of wave mechanics tell us waves move energy through water, causing it to move in a circular motion therefore it does not actually travel with waves. In other words, waves transmit energy, not water, across the ocean and if not obstructed by anything, they have the potential to travel across an entire ocean basin without losing energy.

Similarly, an electromagnetic wave will cause the geometry of space-time to move in a circular motion and therefore the geometric components of space Einstein associated with mass do not move with respect to its velocity vector.

As was just shown the speed of a wave on water is defined in part by the rate at which its particles interact.

Therefore, the reason the speed of light can be defined directly from Maxwells equations is because it is only related to the rate of the interaction of its electrical and magnetic components and not to any other components of space-time.

However, to understand how and why an electromagnetic wave evolves into photon in a space-time environment one must connect its evolution to it.

Again, one can accomplish this by using the science of wave mechanics and the properties of space-time as define by Einstein.

For example, an electromagnetic wave is observed to move continuously through space and time unless it is prevented from doing so by someone or something interacting with it. This would result in its energy being confined to three-dimensional space. The science of wave mechanics tells us the three-dimensional "walls" of this confinement will result in its energy being reflected back on itself thereby creating a resonant or standing wave in three-dimensional space. This would cause its wave energy to be concentrated at the point in space were a particle would be found.

Additionally, wave mechanics also tells us the energy of a resonant system, such as a standing wave can only take on the discrete or quantized values associated with its fundamental or a harmonic of its fundamental frequency.

This explains why an electromagnetic wave if it is prevented from moving through space-time either by being observed or encountering an object is reduced or "Collapses" to a form a standing wave that would define the quantized energy Quantum Mechanics associates with a particle.

This shows how one can define the mathematics of Maxwells equation in terms of the physical properties of space-time

Article 46
The Casmir effect
in space-time.

The Casimir effect is an attractive interaction between two uncharged and perfectly conducting plates held a short distance apart usually less than a micron. Classically, the only attractive force acting between such plates should be gravity. But that's vanishingly small for microscale objects. In 1948 theorist Hendrik Casimir predicted the existence of the force on the scale of a few hundred piconewtons when the plates are held 100 nm apart. This has been observed experimentally many times the force is a nanoscale phenomenon that arises from quantum fluctuations of the electromagnetic vacuum.

Many believe it can **only** be explained by **quantum field theory because it allows** states where the energy between the plates can be arbitrarily negative resulting in a force being developed between them.

However, Einstein provided a classical alternative based on the science of wave mechanics and the observable properties of four-dimensional space-time.

For example, the science of wave mechanics along with the fact that Relativity tells us an electromagnetic wave moves continuously through space-time unless it is prevented from doing so by being observed or interacting with its environment. This would result in its energy being confined to three-dimensional space. The science of wave mechanics also tells us the three-dimensional "walls" of this confinement will result in its energy being reflected back on itself thereby creating a resonant or standing wave in three-dimensional space. **While the distanced between the "walls" of its confinement would be defined the wavelength of its resonate frequency.**

This would cause its wave energy to be concentrated at the point in space were a particle would be found. Additionally, wave mechanics also tells us the energy of a resonant system, such as a standing wave can only take on the discrete or quantized values associated with its fundamental or a harmonic of its fundamental frequency.

However, classical wave mechanics also tells us the number of resonate systems in space-time that could exist between two plates would decreases as the gap between them decreases because the distance between the "plats would define the number of resonant systems that could exist between them.

But it also tells us if the distance between the plates in the Casmir experiment is less than a whole number of the wavelengths associated with the fundamental frequency of the resonant of properties of its environment will result in an "empty" volume of space to exist between the plates. This will create a region which will have negative energy density with respect to the volume associated with the resonant properties of space-time.

This defines an alternative explanation for the Casmir effect and why some regions of space-time can have negative vacuum energy relative to its ordinary vacuum energy.

Additionally, it defines the existence Zero-point energy based on the assumption that space-time has a fundamental resonant frequency. This is because its wavelength would define the minimum volume of space-time that a particle could exist in. Therefore, the lowest energy that could exist in a quantum mechanical or a space-time environment can have because no particles would be able to form in it.

Article 47
Einstein's solution to the horizon problem

The horizon problem is a term given to the fact that the distant regions of space in opposite directions of the sky are so far apart that, assuming standard Big Bang expansion, they could never have been in causal contact with each other enough to allow for the uniform of distribution of matter and energy.

The standard model of cosmology describes the major stages of the evolution of the observable universe, over time. However, it presents problems that constitute a puzzle nowadays. One of them is the horizon problem. The inflationary model, originally introduced by A. Guth in 1981, was designed to solve it. Since then, we are faced now with more than 200 inflationary models.

However, the reason there is are so many models **may be** because there is no way based on observations of our present universe to define **why the big bang happened, when it happened, how long it lasted, the strength of the outward its force, the factor by which the universe expanded and the amount of energy it imparted to matter when it stopped in terms of the observable properties of our universe.**

Yet Einstein gave us a solution to most if not all of those questions based on the observable properties of our universe when he defined gravity in terms of the energy density of space-time.

Cosmologists have not yet determined if the universe will keep on expanding or enter a contraction phase.

However, if it does its energy density and temperature would increase due to its matter and energy being confined to a smaller volume.

One could use that fact to define how a black hole would contribute to its expansion This is because Einstein defined gravity in terms of the differential energy density of space. This means the universe's the energy density increase due to its collapse would result in the event horizon of a black hole to expand outward because the energy differential between it and the surrounding space decreases. This would result in releasing some of its stored energy.

This means as the energy density increased due to the collapse of universe, the event horizon of a black hole would expand because the energy differential between it and the surrounding space decreases. This would result in releasing some of its stored energy to space.

Granted the energy released by the expansion of a single one would have a small effect on the universe.

However, the **cascading** release of energy due to the positive feedback loop created by a large number over a short period of time **would** result in an **exponential** or inflationary increase in its temperature and its expansion rate. In other words, the big bang may not have originated in an "explosion" of quantum singularity as many of the big bang models suggested but an explosion caused by a cascading release of energy from a large number of black holes.

Additionally, one of the **core** principals of relativity is the energy cannot be propagated faster than the speed of light.

This means if the universe did begin as a disassociation of black's holes as was suggested above its energy would not be free to expand at an unlimited speed. Therefore, because energy released from the process mention above would be trapped in an expanding volume define by the speed of light its temperature would increase exponentially.

This may provide a solution to the horizon problem because the components of the universe would be trapped in a relativity small volume giving them enough time to interact with each other as it expanded.

(Some may disagree because of the fact the further we look out in space the faster objects are moving away from us which suggests that space-

time is expanding faster than the speed of light. However, even though that is true the maximum rate of the outward expansion of the universe can still be limited to the speed of light.

This is because the expansion of its surface is defined by πD^2 as its diameter increase. Therefore, even though the rate of change in its diameter is limited to the speed of light, the rate at which surface expands is not but would be define by the square of its diameter or the speed of light.

Putting it another even though Einstein tell us the boundaries of space-time cannot expand faster than the speed of light the **apparent** velocity of points inside of relative to others it can.

One could also estimate **when its expansion happened** or began relative to the present by applying the laws of thermodynamics and Einstein's equations to determine the speed at which energy would be release from a black hole and therefore tell us when that release would be large to prevent further collapse.

Since relativity tells us that the expansion of the universe could **not** have occurred faster than the speed of light one may be able to predict its age by determining how long it would take for its component to interact enough to explain the observed distribution of matter in it

This **would** a define a mechanism to solve the horizon problem because it would provide based on the observation that energy could not have expanded faster that the speed of light for defining a much slower rate of expansion in the beginning than the current models

Article 48
Could Einstein's realization energy can only be propagated at the speed of light solves the Flatness problem

The flatness problem has to do with the geometry of our universe, which appears (especially with recent WMAP evidence) to be a flat. The matter density and expansion rate of the universe appear to be nearly perfectly balanced, even 14 billion years later when minor variations should have grown drastically. The flatness problem as it is called is how to define why this is true.

Many believe it can be solved by assuming during an inflationary period the curvature of the universe neared flatness in the same way as inflating a balloon flattens out regions on its surface. It does so by assuming the volume of space itself expanded by a factor of 10^78 in a fraction of a second. Put another way, the universe might have actually been curved right as it was created

But before we begin, we must first define where the energy responsible for its beginning originated.

Many physics believe it was contained in a singularity which is a place in the universe where our laws of physics simply break down.

However, there is another way which not only is observable quantifiable but is consistent with the laws developed by Einstein

In article 26 (page 136) we discussed Sir Roger Penrose theory known as "Conformal Cyclic Cosmology" in which he postulated the universe has gone through infinite cycles. Briefly he suggested each cycle starts out from a singularity in a Black hole before expanding and generating clumps of matter, which eventually gets sucked up by super massive black holes, which over the very long term disappear by continuously emitting Hawking radiation.

But as was shown in that article there is another way in which black holes could have contributed to its expansion based on General Relativity which does **not** have its origins in a singularity but in rapid release of energy in black holes caused by the increasing energy density of a collapsing universe.

Cosmologists have not yet determined if the universe will keep on expanding or enter a contraction phase.

However, if it does its energy density and temperature would increase due to its matter and energy being confined to a smaller volume.

One could use that fact to define how a black hole would contribute to its expansion This is because Einstein defined gravity in terms of the differential energy density of space. This means as the universe's energy density increase due to its collapse it would result in the event horizon of a black hole to expand outward because the energy differential between it and the surrounding space decreases. This would result in releasing some of its stored energy.

Granted the energy released by the expansion of a single one would have a small effect on the universe.

However, the **cascading** release of energy due to the positive feedback loop created by a large number over a short period of time **would** result in an **exponential** increase in its temperature and its expansion rate.

The science of thermodynamics defines how the universe's energy density would increase as it collapses. This means one could use observations of the present one to estimate if the energy density generated by the momentum of its collapse would become great enough to cause the event horizon of a black hole expand and release its stored energy. Additionally, it would allow one to use those same observations to estimate the temperature at which the expansion began and the rate at which it took place.

One advantage to this is it defines a mechanism for the origins of our current universe in terms of its observable properties and the currently accepted laws of physics. This is because, one can, through observations estimate the total energy content and number of the black holes in the universe at the time its collapse began based on how many presently exist and how many will be created when all of the stars use up their fuel and collapse to one. This would **not only** allow one to estimate the rate of its reexpansion but when it would occur based on their numbers and rate at which their energy would have been released by the process outlined above.

One of the CORE principals of Relativity is energy cannot be propagated faster than the speed of light.

This means if the universe did begin as a release of a black's holes energy as was suggested above its energy would **not** be free to expand at an unlimited speed. Therefore, the energy released from the process mentioned above would be trapped in a volume defined by the speed of light.

As was mentioned earlier the inflation model solves the flatness by assuming the volume of space expanded by a factor of 10^78 in a fraction of a second.

However as was shown above one can define a mechanism that suggests our universe may have expand at a much slower rate over much greater time period based on the current laws of physics and the observation that energy cannot be propagated faster the speed of light than is suggested by the Big Bang and many other models' theoretical models.

The above mechanism for the origin of our universe would solve the Flatness problem because matter and energy would not be free to expand but confined to a small volume that could only expand at the speed of light. This would give matter and energy time to adjust themselves to fit the dimensional properties of the universe imposed by the velocity of light. This because Einstein showed they are determined by the speed of light its matter and energy would interact to conform to it thereby eliminating any small deviations from this critical value which would have resulted in a curved universe today. Additionally, the relationship between matter and energy in the universe is dependent on the constant speed of light it will remain constant throughout its history

Sources

NASA

CERN

European space agency

Department of Energy, Office of Science

Stanford Encyclopedia of Philosophy

Physics world

Scientific America

New Scientist

Made in the USA
Columbia, SC
29 July 2025